GW00357250

It's A Funny World

It's a
FUNNY
world

Hilary Heyer

The Book Guild Ltd
Sussex, England

The Book Guild Ltd
25 High Street,
Lewes, Sussex

First published 1994
© Hilary Heyer 1994

Set in Palacio

Typesetting by Formaprint, Worthing

Printed in Great Britain by
Antony Rowe Ltd.
Chippenham, Wiltshire.

A catalogue record for this book is available
from the British Library

ISBN 0 86332 893 8

CONTENTS

1
GOOD GUIDE TO CREATIVE MOANING

I Peddle Laughter

'No,' I answered, 'I am not a writer, I am a pedlar. I peddle laughter'

I am one of those poor pedlars of that very rare commodity called laughter. One of those funny people who collects laughs and chuckles and cheers like a magpie would collect bright and shiny objects. For ever looking for the funny side of life, for ever trying to turn all those sour lemons of life into some sort of sweet lemonade of jollity.

Very much needed, you will say, humour and laughter, in this vale of tears.

Are you joking? Do you know how bad business is in Life's Laughing Department? Dead — I am telling you — as dead as a dead herring's tail. So dead in fact, that I am seriously thinking of opening some sort of discount operation. Like a dollar per ten chuckles and four giggles for the price of one.

I can hear some kind-hearted soul exclaim: 'Come off it! Surely nobody has to sell humour at a discount? After all, everybody wants to be cheered up with a chuckle or two, sometime or other.'

You want to bet? Ever tried to greet a gloomy face with a cheerful 'Good morning!' and see what happens? Some can hardly squeeze, 'morning' never mind 'good'; and some just bark at you 'What's so good about it?!' and leave you as cheerless as that dead herring's tail.

Or again, have you ever tried to cheer up a friend? And what do you get? A major explosion — like a pressure cooker all gone p-s-s-t and pop. 'Cheer me up?' she explodes, 'with my kids? Screaming my eardrums out of my head? And all those blinking gadgets going on the blink; and me, going like a loonie, round and round in town looking for a parking place till I am ready to climb the nearest telegraph pole; and you want me to cheer up?'

See what I mean? Very few of us really wants to be

9

cheered up. And yet — I am sure you'll agree — if there is one thing we need more than all the gold in the Reserve Bank and all the diamonds in Kimberley is that little bit of good cheer and that little bit of laughter, just to lighten a little all those life's trials and tribulations.

Because, really, we do take life far too seriously. Just look at any crowd. With all those tight lips and droopy chins, drooping half way down the chest, all looking like so many un-cheer-uppable undertakers. I tell you, if a Martian landed in the middle of it all, he'd take one jiffy look at this miserable lot and turbo-boost back into the sky — pronto!

Now I know there will be lots of glum gloomies who will croak, 'In this world of gloom and doom, what is there to laugh about?'

To this I say you'll be amazed how many funny sides there are — even to the gloomiest doom, if only we cared to look for it. But for the time being let us dig into my little goldmine of cheers galore. All you have to do is relax with a cuppa or a glass of vino and be my kindred spirit (non-bottle variety).

But I must warn you — cheeky devil, me — prices are going up and next time it'll be two dollars per chuckle and no discount for this (pardon the brag) delightfully lighthearted banter.

P.S. And lastly, I forgot to tell you — I am a professional Grumble Bag, registered at the Post Office No. XYZ/707 — for a bit of mystery! Turn the page and come with me to explore that sadly unexplored world of my Comic Muse, where there is always laughter in your every tear.

Down with Doom Mongers!

Believe it or not — the doom mongers are at it again. This time about Haley's comet. One says: Imagine forty moons lined up, side to side, right across the sky! Another says: A comet with that size tail can only mean an ill omen. Plague, carnage and pestilence. And another smart astroaleck blubbers: if you are a Libra (which I am), watch out for the dust from the mid-tail of the comet Haley. It can affect your — guess what — sex life!

Before that mid-tail astrodust finally falls — and ruins my sex life — I feel I must hurry up and say my piece about all those doomsday scares and get it off my chest — once and for all.

I want to say, Down with Doom Mongers!

I want to tell all those high-falutin celestial-ists and -'ologists that I have quite enough to worry about, what with all the floods and droughts, my knock-knees and my ingrown toes, my hubby's egg-bald pate and my sleeping partner who never sleeps (I mean the taxman). Believe you me, I have more than enough to worry about.

I don't want to worry on top of it about Green Men from the Red Planet, world's roof rising and world's bottom falling out, asteroids colliding and black holes gulping stars, quarks and quasars and ten-ton space junk that's supposed to crash-bang into my petunia patch — but never does.

All of which adds up to my fervent plea: Please scientists — give me a break, for about 100 years at least — and stop scaring me with all those dooms that never doom.

Like the last one, a couple of years ago, remember? When the world was going to end. Honestly — it turned me into fifty nine and a half kilos of spastic jelly for three days before the day. And on the day — I tell you — I was so petrified I hid myself in one of those cubic holes above the built-in wardrobe, hoping that being packed in a small space, I'd arrive at the Pearly Gates in one piece instead of in

11

hundreds of smithereens; my big toe in Timbuctoo and my thumb in somebody's curry soup in Calcutta. But actually what scared me out of my skin was a. . . . cockroach. A he-cockroach chasing a she-cockroach up my pyjama legging. Boy, oh boy — did I jump — like a supersonic bullet on two legs!

Needless to say, as always, doom was no nigher. But I know that as soon as I relax after one scare, another will be on the go. It's as if there were some frustrated Frankestein declaring with glee, Now, this old hag (me) has had enough peace and tranquility for twelve moons or more. Time we scared her out of her wits again. This time we'll roast her in Lunar Quarks (to be invented at a later date!)

Don't We Love Our Lu-ver-ly Grumbles!

Aren't some people born gloomies? Try cheering them up and they bark back, 'What is there to be cheerful about?' And yet, life is full of laughter — if you only look for it. Me, I forever look for some anti-gloom game. For example, You know that song from *My Fair Lady*, 'Wouldn't it be luverly?' I use it to make up my own funny list of 'wouldn't it be lu-ver-lies.'

Wouldn't it be luverly if some Mr Big Cigar declared, 'Our poor housewife — honestly — my heart bleeds for her! Walking her toes to the bone, chasing those 3p DOWN on a tin of peas, only to find 6p UP on ditto pilchards. This must stop forthwith. I now proclaim this year our Non-Profit Year. When absolutely everything goes a-b-s-olutely free!'

And if we had no petrol problems forever looming. If your petrol tank and your radiator miraculously changed places. So you could put water into your petrol tank and just a weeny dash of petrol in your radiator — just once a year. Imagine the bliss and prosperity! The sheiks could go back to the harems and the world back to sanity.

And if metermaids got fed up with *us* (instead of us being fed up with them) and they all went on strike. So we could all park anywhere, free — a day at a stretch.

And if your boss said, 'Work? You don't have to work anymore. Not even collect your money. We'll send you a cheque on the 30th — no problem. Wouldn't that be just lu-ver-ly? With no food, fuel or work problems — and money to burn — we could laze our lives away, lolling on a lilo in the swimming pool. Perfect bliss!

But alas — it wouldn't last long. Soon we'd all be grumbling. About life so crushingly boring, without a single grumble to utter.

And it would be. For imagine — never to cry, 'Work — whoever invented it ought to have been shot!' And,

'Parking — it's mu-urder!' And, 'isn't it terrible how you save 3p on peas and lose 6p on pilchards!' Imagine missing all these lu-ver-ly grumbles? Plain un-bearable!

For the truth of the matter is — much as we hate to admit it — we like grumbling. It's the only thing in the world we get a-b-s-olutely free!

Le Laughter And Le Moan

You just can't help but laugh! When you think what a funny business is this business of laughter. How a joke can make you ab-so-lutely collapse with laughter and yet — all it gives your friend is one big hippo-wide yawn. So true of all humour, isn't it? One man's chuckle is another man's yawn.

And while on the subject, listen to what one French doctor says about laughter. In franglais of course.'LE laughter,' the good doctor says, 'improves LE circulation, expands LE blood vessels, deepens LE breathing, speeds LE wound healing — and believe it or not — helps you to exercise LE 100 muscles every time you laugh.'

So there you have it. Even science now says, Keep laughing! LE good laugh is LE good tonic.

But I tell you something else: LE good moan is even better. You know the kind? That long l-o-n-g moan. When you moan till you cry, and you cry till you can cry no more, till in the end all you can do is just burst out laughing. And that — the good doctor says — is LE best laughter of them all. It gives you — guess how many? — 107 muscles' exercise — no kidding — 107 — including your eyelashes!

So, if you ever need a good cheerer-upper, just pick your chewiest moan and chew and chew at it till you can roar with laughter and that — the good doctor says — is the best therapy in the world — laughotherapy.

But what if you have so many moans that you can't choose the chewiest? Have a standby moan that you can always fall back on. Something that will make you cry yourself silly and laugh yourself sore.

Like I do. I never even have to look for a moan now. I have a standard one lined up, day or night. If you were to shake my shoulder at 4 a.m. and ask me what's my moan, I tell you, I'd shoot my moan like a shot and droll it out like a hypnotised zombie: My dearly beloved, my

Macho Moustache, that's my moan. Was, is, and will be for e-t-ernity!

Why is this Macho Moustache such a mega-moan? you'll ask. Ah, now — that's another very sad and sorry story.

Laugh With One Eye
While Crying With The Other

Three cheers for Mr Davis, the editor of *Punch* who says we badly need to sharpen our sense of humour.

I agree, but think that it applies to all of us, all over the globe. We need 'a laugh a day keeps the doctor away' campaign — universally, to see ourselves as, say a man from the Moon would see us. And what a roar that would be!

Because, really, some of the funny things we do! For example, how we slog and slave to make money, only to find we haven't any time — or energy for — what we have been slaving for. And how we go on holidays to 'get away from it all' — and then cart along with us that very 'all' we were so desperate to get away from.

Or take our mighty science. How we can devise the most ingenious computers and yet can't invent a pen that doesn't leak or a simple zip that doesn't get stuck.

Or how we can land a moon buggy on the moon, by remote control, without a single hitch. And yet — two planes can collide in mid-air just where you would have thought there was enough airspace for a million of zeppelins!

All of which makes me want to laugh with one eye while crying with the other. And this is the kind of humour that we need most.

If you agree, turn the page and have a chuckle that cheers!

Vot, No Var? Mamma Mia!

People! Really, some-a-times I could a-scream! Take my name, for example. Now my name is Pellita Dellici, half Italian, half German and threequarters universal — if you know what I mean. But they all call me Mamma Mia. Because they say if I say ten words seven of them would be Mamma Mia. But — if they had my life's hassles and hardsheeps, they would -a-scream Mamma Mia ten out ten!

Because hassles! I got plenty for da universe. What with my dolce Benito ('nuff said) and da kids; add to that da cooking — three times a day every day, because they all want to eat three times a day EVERY day; add to that traffic jams and traffic cops and all da million other mod monsters — and I tell you, it's a miracle how me no go crazy. A miraKEL! Mamma Mia!!

To which my dolce Benito says, 'If you go on bustin' and burstin' with all these Mamma Mias, one day you go bust and kaput and there'll be no Pellita — and what's Benito without Pellita?

But I don't-a-care. Right now I feel like a pressure cooker, ready to p-s-s-t and burst and hit da ceiling. With all dis war beeziness.

Because I mean, Mamma Mia, — five billion million years we fight and fight and war and war and — war! And we learn nix and nil and zero. Since Hiroshima we've had 125 wars — 125! Mamma Mia! Like-a some keeds playing cowboys and Injuns and ah bunch of let-a-loose lunatix! And with all these desperadoes of da universe out to biff all the other desperadoes, I am telling you — a bomb can land in my garlic patch quicker than I can say Mamma Mia. Just-a-there--gedung!

My dolce Benito has a twist to this pressure cooker p-s-s-t. He says, 'Just imagine for uno momento all wars finito. No demos, terrists, highjackers or kid-a-nappers. Ruskies no fight Yankies, Commies no fight capitalists. And Pellita no fight Benito.'

Just imagine — Mamma Mia! La dolce vita wouldn't be very dolce, would it? If I could never love uno momento and hate next momento. And never know da sweet kiss of sorry. I tell you — when that happens, Pellita will be fi-nito!

Because never to love and never to hate is never to laugh. And me, Pellita, I must-a laugh. Me no laugh, me die.

Down With Perfect Weatheritis!

It's no joke this weather business. For weeks now it's been like a yo-yo, blazing hot and freezing cold. Till sometimes I feel like an onion on two legs. Piling on seven layers of clothes in the morning, only to peel off six of them by noon. Recently I've had some pretty thunderbolt clashes with my scientist husband over who is to blame. I say — you've guessed it — it's the scientists. And he says I have the anti-ist and anti-ologist bug on my brain. In fact, I ought to join the crowd of the same ilk: the Flat Earth Society.

But I still insist it's the bomb. And who invented it? The scientists. Or take the airosol, that anti-pong psst can. It has apparently increased carbon dioxide sevenfold, is about to melt half the Antarctic ice cap and raise the sea three metres up. And who, pray, invented that? Once again the scientists. Add to that all that cloud seeding and trillions of sattelites snooping (done by an army of -ist snoopers) and I tell you, Mother Nature rebels. She says, I'll show you who is the boss. And thirty degrees drops to five, Sahara sandstorms hit London and poor Eskimos sizzle like so much whale blubber.

But whenever I get ths anti-ist brainstorm, my comic Imp, the great debunker whispers, Try and see the other side. Just imagine, never to say "Uh, the weather!" and "Oh, for a spot of sunshine or a spot of rain!" And never to be able to blame the weather for all those funny moods of ours. And most of all, never to be able to start a conversation with "What a funny weather we've been having/have had/ are having!"

Well, I mean - it doesn't bear thinking, does it?

Can you imagine 365 days of nothing but sunshine? Just perfect weather — the monotony of it! I can hear on the news, 'sixteen out of twenty factories are closing down and hundreds of workers are down with a mysterious disease called Perfect Weatheritis.'

And you know what will follow? No colds and no 'flu. What would happen to us poor creatures who depend on colds and flu to keep us going?

Like me for example. For years I've always blamed this common foe for all sorts of ills of flesh and spirit. Whenever I felt sick of my job, my boss, my husband or my kids — anything and anybody — you could bet your last aspro I'd blame the cold. It was for ever coming or going, with me for ever catching it. But with a perfect weather, what would I blame now?

It sure is a funny world!

Good Guide To Creative Moaning

Want a chuckle or two to cheer up your day? Then come and meet my great buddy I've shared many a tear of laughter with, that great cheerer-upper, Misery Mona.

Misery Mona says, My best moans waft my way while I am beautifying myself in front of my bathroom mirror. So, my friend, see me now, trying to curl up this darn unruly curler (pink) while I am doing what comes naturally — moaning.

And now for a little humble brag-brag here. You see, I've always been good at that, I mean moaning. What I can't moan about is simply not worth moaning about!

Then one day — one of those Date with Destiny days — I had a brilliant brainwave. Why not be a professional and specialise in moaning? And that's how I became a celebrity, world's first Moan and Groan specialist. By now, no kidding, I have a collection of 4,996 moans of all sorts. Mini, midi, maxi and any old size in between. Name your moan and that's my moan too.

All I need now is just four more moans to 5,000 (world record) and then guess what I am going to do? Write my best seller, *My Good Guide To Creative Moaning*. Now, don't you start sniggering out there! Because I mean if that Bozo Boy George can sell his best seller, *A Good Guide to Sex and Scandal*, and make a cool million, by Jove, so can I!

And what will the message be in that. . . err . . .best seller? A MOAN A DAY KEEPS THE DOCTOR AWAY!

Good moaning motto, eh? Now, I bet you are itching to know what will be my Numero Uno in my famous Moan Collection? I'd love to tell you my friend, you must believe me. But, while curling up that unruly curler (pink) I had another brilliant brainwave. Warning me: Are you crazy? Have you no sense of suspense? Don't you know suspense is the spice of life that keeps our vital (laughing) juices atingling? Just keep curling that darn unruly curler (pink) and for mercy sake, keep'em guessing! Keep them suspended in sus-pense!

So until our next moaning session, here is me, Misery Mona, wishing you and yours: Happy Moaning!

Peddling Those Tearful Chuckles

I bet you'll be surprised to hear what I am peddling now. Chuckles, my friend — and at a discount rate. Yea, be shocked. That's what we poor chuckle pedlars have been reduced to. Selling at a discount rate. Four chuckles for the price of one.

What sort of chuckles? you'll ask. All sorts, my friend; all sorts of anti-gloom and anti-doom and anti- all those beastly blues. That's what chuckles.

And the first one — going-going-gone — is that funny item about those peculiar statistics. For example, how they say that out of every hundred people, ninety three and a half per cent get regularly depressed. Now, to my mind-this half per cent must surely mean half a Joe or half a Joan. Which in turn must mean that right now there is somebody — some Joe or some Joan — walking about with just one arm, one leg, half a head and one eye depressed. While the rest of him/her is all tra-la-la happy!

I certainly could not qualify for that half depressed body. Because when I am depressed you can be sure I am a full-bodied depressed body. Guaranteed. Down to my big toe and up to my left eyelash, depressed body.

And what do I get depressed about, right up to my left eyelash? Well now — that's just it, my friend. Have a chuckle on me here. Because more often than not I haven't a clue what I am depressed about. And it's no good you asking me how can I be depressed if I don't even know what I am depressed about. I just am. Depressed.

Like I was the other day. I can chuckle about it now — post factum — but oh, was I right down in those proverbial dumps, uh! So down in fact, that if I stepped one step downer, you know where I would have ended? Right in the bowels of this unjolly mudball — somewhere in Patagonia!

And you know what gets me then? When I am in those

Patagonia 'whatsits'? Those cheerer-uppers. Uh, those cheerer-uppers, for ever chirping, 'Cheer up, cheer up — it isn't that bad!' And my reply always is, 'It's not that bad, because it's worse than bad. And more often than not too.

And next? next is that motley crew, the shaker-outers. For ever jabbering, 'Shake yourself out of it! Shake yourself out of it!' Shake myself out of it! As if I was a dusty carpet shaking its dust out of itself. I mean, have a heart! How can you shake yourself out of yourself when there is nothing left there to shake!

Believe you me, my friend, I tried this shaking myself out of myself once at a dinner party. When I shook myself a shake too vigorously and you know what happened? I lost my false eyelash — no kidding — Magnifico de Luxe it was too. Plonk it went into this hot mess called Muligatawny soup.

But what really slays me are those twits that twitter, 'What you need to do' says she, 'is find out exactly what depresses you!' Sometimes I feel like crying 'What depresses me? It's not *what* depresses me, it is *who* depresses me and I know exactly *who* that *who* is. My dearly beloved, — that's who. Lovingly nicknamed by me my Macho Moustache. Because — boy oh boy, can he depress me, this male gender whatsit — you've no idea!'

But that's another story.

Meet The Worrynut Supremo

Now you might think that I am trying to pull your leg, but I am not, cross my Christian heart, I am not. Because I actually heard about this exciting happening on the news. In that very special slot where they tell you all about snakes getting flu and crocs getting dentures. You know the one I mean? Where Prince Charles did his breakdance and all that jazz?

Now in that very slot a couple of days ago there was this priceless bit of news about this enterprising fellow in New York who wants to organise a competition for all the people who can worry — and make a good job of it. Sort of worry, worry, worry till death do us part type of worrynut. So that at the end of it the judges can declare that champion of champions, the worry champ of the world — to be known from then on as the Worrynut of the World, 1991.

And if you dont believe me now, I can assure you, you soon will. Because it's bound to be on the eleven o'clock news again, sooner or later. In that very special slot where they show you all those snakes getting flu and all those crocs getting dentures. Then you'll see it for yourself, how the entries are pouring in, by the thousand, already. From all four corners of the globe — if not five!

Now I know you are going to ask me why I am giving you all this preview of a preview to a preview. Because I want to warn you my friend, that's why. Just in case you are good at worrying, in which case you might think of entering this f-a-bulous competition. So let me warn you right now. Don't waste your time worrying about it, or practising all that worry, worry, worry for that championship. Because — I know for a fact — you'll never make it. Take it from me, you don't stand a chance. And do you know why? Simply because you — are you still listening? — simply because you have the biggest giant of a competitor there ever was, is or will be. In the worrying business I mean. Who? you ask. How can you ask, Who? Me, of course.

You can hear the trumpets already, can't you? Triumphantly blazing away in all their glory; proclaiming to the world that first and best worrynut of the world.

How can I be so sure? Well, I mean — it's very simple. What I don't know about worrying is simply not worth worrying about!

I know you will ask: Any hints from the Worrynut Supremo? How to worry yourself to death — and stay half dead? Ah, now, that's another story, for another time.

Optimist v. Pessimist

Here is a chuckle to cheer you up — an amusing quip about optimist v. pessimist. It says, 'Twixt optimist and pessimist the difference is droll, the optimist sees the doughnut and the pessimist the hole.'

But even better illustration is that popular tale about two men and a tumbler of water. Two men are lying side by side in a hospital, both recovering from the same op and each has a tumbler of crystal clear water on his locker. One man — we'll call him Cheerful Charlie — takes a sip, then a deeper gulp and then, beating his chest with delight, he proclaims, 'L-l-lovely water!'

But to the other man, old Grumpy Guts, to him nothing is ever lovely, least of all hospital water! Taking only a mini sip, as if it was some poison, he spits and splatters and scorns with utmost disgust. 'What a f-o-ul stuff!' Then he pops a pink pill into the water, making it sickly sweet, and next a yellow pill that makes it bitter and lastly a chocolate-coated one. By which time you can imagine the water has churned into a murky mudpool and old Grumpy Guts explodes with a battery of grumbles. All about the hospital and the foul water and of course the doctors. 'These quacks!' he perorates, 'they poison you, you know that?'

Absolutely. I bet they are all in cahoots with those them undertakers!

Despite all this grumble galore, our Cheerful Charlie manages to crack a joke or two with the staff, write three 'thank you' cards and is now in the middle of his 'howdy' letter to his best buddy. Chuckling, he writes, 'You should see my companion here, the biggest grumble on two legs that's ever walked God's earth! I swear he must be in cahoots with the undertakers! because boy, — can he grumble! You should hear him now. Prostrate like a corpse, and groaning, Help! Help! — I am d-y-ing!!'

I don't have to tell you who will leave the hospital first.

the optimist of course. And it's the optimist who will find it easier to pass exams , find a job, open a business or further any career of his choice simply because he looks for the good in life and what he looks for he finds.

So, whenever you get tempted to be a Grumpy old Guts remember that, like all of us, you are given a tumbler of Life and it's up to you to make it into a fountain of joy and energy instead of polluting it with negative, pessimistic and mostly imaginary grumbles. Try and use your energy, your time and most of all your imagination to help you to live and not to provide jobs for undertakers — long before your time!

2

THE TRIALS OF EVERYDAY LIFE

Early To Bed — I Ask You!

It sure is a funny world, full of funny proverbs. Like this one for example all the killjoys just love croaking about: Early to bed and early to rise makes a man healthy, wealthy and wise.

I ask you — have you ever heard such utter nonsense in your life before? To my mind it's not only nonsense, it's an out and out lie. Because have you ever seen a man who looks healthy when he is rudely yanked out of his cosy bed at the crack of dawn?

I haven't. On the contrary, he looks quite the opposite — positively sick. With one eye half closed and the other firmly shut and with his mouth corners hanging somewhere on his chest, he can hardly squeeze 'Morning' leave alone Good. And if you ask him what's the matter, he will tell you it makes him sick to get up in the morning.

But compare him with a hubby on holiday, after a long lie-in and a leisurely breakfast at the civilised hour of 10.30 mid-morning, — and see the difference. He brims with health and vitality and bursts with *joie de vivre*. Beating his chest with delight, he proclaims, 'Boy, I feel good. It's good to be alive!'

Or take farmers who seem to spend their lives competing with the cockerel — always up before dawn. By the proverb's rule they ought to be millionaires many times over. But they aren't. Instead who gets stinking rich? The middleman who never sees the crack of dawn in his whole life!

Or take labourers — those poor souls who have to get up before sunrise — day in day out, heatwave or hail. Have you ever heard them going to work and whistling, 'Happiness is . . . getting up early in the morning? Of course not. The only time they *do* whistle is when they go back home from work. Then they sigh, 'Oh, for that l-uverly bed! And they certainly aren't wealthy. The boss is,, who believes in, 'Late to bed and late to rise makes you wealthy.' To him only a fool cares about being wise.

But it's my old friend, Sid, who puts it all in a nutshell when he says, 'What I'd like to know is who first coined this nugget of wisdom. Some killjoy, I bet — back in 1066.' I can hear him now drawling out, 'Early to rise . . . now what will rhyme with early to rise? Healthy, wealthy and wise.' And so — for ten centuries after that we all go croaking, 'Early to rise, early to rise . . .' Uh, the very thought of it makes me shiver. If I had my way, I tell you — I'd have that silly proverb abolished, universally — by public discontent!!

You Can't Help But Miss It!

It sure is a funny world — full of paradoxes — like this one for examaple: how modern man can land on the moon and yet he can't direct you to the next dorp.

If anything, he is sure to *mis*-direct you. For he either showers you with first turn-lefts and second turn-rights till you almost don't know which is your right hand and which is your left; or shoots at you names of streets and crossings till you forget which street you wanted in the first place. And always ending, 'That's easy. You can't miss it, if you tried!'

To me it's, 'Easy, ha, ha' more likely. Now over the years I've collected quite a list of these 'Easy, ha, ha's' — and some of them, really, they deserve to be immortalised for posterity. Like this decimal genius, your genuine kilometer into centimeter splitter. He just l-o-ves telling you, 'Turn right at 500m., then go on for 300m., then turn left and go on for 100m. He would have ended with, then stop at 1m. 11cm, — if you stopped to listen. Which to me is worse than driving with a metre of alcohol in my arteries. Because I'd be so dead tense I'd be sure to end 10 cm. from the first telegraph pole — or worse!

Then there is this rare bird, the grit and grout specialist who knows more about gritted chippings and grouted macadams than all the AA men put together. 'Now go for two kms on this paving block,' says this expert, 'then turn right onto the ferro-concrete. But be careful, it's the grouted macadam you want and not the tar with gritted chippings.' All very impressive, I am sure. But what this fellow forgets is that I wouldn't know grit from grout if Mercedes Benz was the quiz prize for knowing it. All I know is tarmac, not even macadam.

Then, of course, there is your detail devotee who prides himself on knowing all the ins and outs of his locality better than you know the nose on your face. Like the Andy Capp type of cockney who once in London tried to direct me to Sterling Street. 'That's easy, luv. See that cloud on the horizon and a church spire with three tiles missing? Pass that and look for the ONE EYED RED BULL pub, with the bull's eye black and a funny little eyelash flicking at you and then. . .Then, you've guessed it — I went smack wallop into a red London double decker.

But the first prize in this 'Easy, ha, ha,' contest belongs — naturally — to our friend in all our traffic trials and tribulations — the traffic cop. Now this happened once when I had to catch a night plane and there was this officious ramrod of a cop drawling out, 'Proceed to the next crossing.' Only to find the cop there drawling out, 'Proceed back to the last crossing.' And after I had done a couple of these back and forth 'proceedings', guess what the first cop said, 'L-a-a-dy,' he said, 'are you playing some kind of cops-n-robbers game or something?'

All of which adds up to what my motorist friend says: 'They all say it's easy, you can't miss it if you tried, And yet you always do. You can't help *but* miss it.

The Loony McLoonen Machine

Our Misery Mona (she of the 4000 moans) says:

I don't want to alarm you my friend, but I feel I'd be failing in my duty as a non-loony visionary if I didn't raise this alarming alarum. It was so alarming when I heard it first that my bottom jaw dropped where my chest is and stayed there for the duration. All I could do is cry, A-m-azing!

So here is my alarum: there are some disturbing goings-on afoot (or rather awheel) in today's racing world. We all know that in motor racing speed is of the essence, that the racing fundis are for ever 'souping up' their McLarens and breaking new records with milliseconds precision. Till now most of us cry, Where will it all end? All this more and more kms in less and less millisecs?

I tell you where. In that ultimate neck-breaker, that mean machine called McLoonen, that's where.

And it is here that your bottom jaw will drop and stay dropped, like mine did, when you hear the Great McLoonen story.

Recently released report by designer, Herr Bruno Krakkenpotten, in the mag *MotorBiz* says, At long last ve haf ze lift-off. Our McLoonen Speed Ace can compete met wind and met McLaren. Even met Space Challenger.

It even looks like it, like a whopper pencil. Zo long (3m 28cm) and zo narrow in ze front (69,075 cm), there is room for *one* knee only.

Asked how is the racer going to race — kneeling on one knee, Herr Krakkenpotten replied, 'Doing the splitzen, that's how. One leg to ze front and one to ze back.'

'But now,' continued the genius, 'we have hitten on a major hitch. And do not laughen, it's the sneeze.

'You see with this 'splitzen' position — one leg to the front and one to the back — the balance is z-o critical, the slightest shake can upset the delicate fulcrum of the

37

machinen, even the sneezen.

'During last trial one champ he sneezen and hitten and smashen the grandstanden.'

So now the sneeze test is in progress, trying to get the champs to sneeze *before* and not during the race.

So there you have it, McLoonen 'splitzen' story. You can, of course, do what you will with this alarming info. But don't tell me I haven't warned you. That your present car might soon be obsolete and your next might well be the newest McLoonen Splitzen design — one knee to the front and one knee to the back.

Am I pulling your knee? Don't be silly. Would I pull your leg or your knee when the very safety of your sneeze — and your knees — is in danger?

TV Trivialities

Do you ever get that small voice — your alter ego — buzzing in your ear, telling you what's wrong with you? I often do. I call it my Comic Imp — a great cheerer-upper that helps me to laugh at life with one eye, while crying with the other.

But oh, sometimes it's a perfect pest! The other day it chided, 'Time you stopped this crying with one eye and laughing with the other and started crying proper — with both eyes.

'Over yourself. Because, really, you are the most inconsistent creature on earth. Take TV, for example, How you for ever cry, "What trivial trivialities! What banal banalities!" And how you for ever vow, "That's the last time I watch A-Team, Dallas, Rip Tide!" True?

'And yet, you go on watching it, don't you? Religiously. I can bet my last giggle, come 9.33 p.m. you'll be goggling that goggle box again; chew-chewing with your eyes all those trivial trivialities and banal banalities. In fact, be honest, it has now become your choice chewing gum for your eyes, and your mind- hasn't it?

'But that isn't all. What beats my laughter hollow is how you pontificate about TV and all the evils therof. "It's the death of our creativity," you cry. We have now become so conditioned to this chew-chew-chewing of any old rubbish on TV, we have no time for anything creative. Till eventually, our skills — hand and head — will atrophy: For what you don't use, you lose. And time will come, -you prophesy- when even that TV screen will go blank. Saying: "We have a problem. Nobody wants to write, produce, direct even those bang-bang banalities." These are your own words, true?

Truer than true, I had to admit. 'Comic Imp,' I cried, 'this time you really make me cry. But can we please postpone this tragi-comic tirade for twenty nine minutes? I only have one minute left to get ready . . . for RipTide!'

I Have Contracted Cellophan-itis!

Hello there, my friend — I hope this time you'll have lots of tissue hankies handy (baby bottom softs), because my friend, I have such a sorry story to tell — and no kidding this time!

Poor me, guess what — I've contracted some strange form of -itis. The doctor tells me it's Cellophanitis. Can't face another scrap of wrapping paper, plastic, Cellophane, even paper bags. The moment I see any wrapping material I run into the nearest corner, curl up like a piece of Sellotape, and cry.

It gets me worst on Fridays — my shopping day. I seem to get such an Everest of wrappings. All those packs and packets and mini and maxi boxes. The mini-er the box, the maxi-er the wrapping.

And those paper bags! Those little paper bags that get put into bigger paper bags that get put into still bigger paper bags. Last Friday — cross my christian heart and my future pacemaker! — half of what I brought home was wrapping.

But the last straw was the box of laxatives. You wouldn't believe it, but those unjolly beans were first wrapped individually in foil wrapping; then put into a metal box and sellotaped tightly; then the assistant wrapped that box in brown paper and sellotaped that. Then she put it into a small paper bag and then — crown it all — into a big plastic carrier bag with the firm's name on it. When I unwrapped tha bundle of joy, I just flopped on my weekly rubbish heap and wept, with both eyes!

My friend says it might have been worse. Be glad they are not wrapping each individual brown bean and haricot bean and spotted-dotted bean — for your soup — in sellotaped, cellophaned wrapping. See the funny side of it!

I think I am losing my funny side fast!

P.S. Which sorry story above inspired me to compose — wait for it — a poem.

The very next day after I had bought a shirt for my . . .
worse half.
What do you think of that? Here is how it goes

Wrap Is The Root

As I unwrapped a shirt I'd bought
And was about to throw away its useless wrap:
   One plastic hanger, three plastic studs,
   A cardboard back,
   A Cellophane wrap,
   A cardboard box,
I suddenly thought: Three million shirts have been bought
Today — three million! Lord! And to each there was:
   One plastic hanger, three plastic studs,
   A cardboard back,
   A Cellophane wrap,
   A cardboard box,
   A paper bag —
A whole Mount Everest of wrap!
It hit me then: this is what pollution is about.

I Married A Junk Addict

Some couples have funny marital problems. A couple I know for example differ over which way the lawn should be mown. The man says up and down. And the woman says round and round, around the flower bed in the middle. they have been going in circles over this — for years!

Another couple talk only through their cat, Sooty. Every time he wants his socks mended, he says, 'Sooty, tell your mistress I have a whopper potato hole in my sock.' And she replies, 'Sooty, ask your master what does he do with his socks? Chew them for his dessert?'

But however gigantic other couples' problems are, I still think mine is a ginormous jumbo of a headache. And the short and long of it is: I married a junk addict.

He simply cannot resist any broken pipe, bent nail, rusty screw, hook, lock or one-legged plug that he thinks might come in handy. He never stops to think when. In 1999 or never it's quite immaterial to him. When I ask him what can he possibly do with a smashed car lamp 1953 vintage or a tricycle wheel smashed to a pulp, he always says: You never know!

So — you can well imagine — there is half a ton of this 'you never know' junk about the place. It wouldn't be so bad if he only hoarded his own junk — heaven knows there's enough of that! But he actually goes and *buys* somebody else's junk, at sales and auctions. Can you believe it!

The other day, he came back from town as excited as if he had found a Kohinoor diamond lying on the street. 'Guess what I found?' he cried. It was one of those 'His Master's Voice' battered gramophone tubes — 1922 vintage.

You may laugh, but it's not a laughing matter, I assure you. What has brought it to a head for me is that we are supposed to be moving next month. And every time I phone a removal firm, same thing happens. They send a man to survey the job and the fellow takes one look at the junk and says, 'What you need, madam, is a . . . scrap merchant!

Now do you see my marital dilemma: I don't want to get rid of my husband and I can't get rid of his junk!

Who Is Whose Mob?

People, really, what's the matter with them all? Don't they ever eat or sleep or cook or rest? Because all they seem to be doing — the whole moblot of them — is following me, wherever I go.

But forever, honestly. I haven't a weeniest nook of privacy in this whole wide world. Like of a Sunday for example. I often like to jump into my jalopy and buzz off to the hills, just to get away from it all. But no sooner do I find a secluded spot and sigh, 'Ah, solitude at last!' — there they are, the city hordes, all trailing behind me. And if I glare at them to say, 'Go away, this is *my* retreat!' they glare back at me — the cheek of it — as if that hill was *their* property!

I ask you. Or me and my old square would go for a spot of fishing on a long weekend. And we just settle down in some heavenly nookie, feeling like Adam and Eve must have felt in paradise — oh, so happy — when bang! A great big sedan rolls up with five screaming kids. All wanting to tickle that very fish I am about to tickle. As if there was just that one stream with just that one fish to tickle in the whole world.

As for shopping I tell you — it's MMMurder! And all because they simply won't shop in side streets, this motley mob. They always must shop wherever I shop, in the city centre. And always on Saturday — that's my other gripe. Why not Monday to Friday, when they could buy out the bally town lock, stock and wine barrel? But no, not them, the selfish lot. And if I change it to Mondays — you,ve guessed it — they change it to Mondays too. Uncanny, isn't it? As if they were in some tinkling cahoots, ringing their bosom buddies: The old grumble bag is in town again. Let's go and hassle and bustle and jostle her, just for the heck of it!

My friends say, Come off it, you old grumble bag, you

enjoy the moan. Well, maybe I do. But the point is, if this goes on, there won't be any 'me' left to enjoy the moan!

Like last holiday queuing for a movie ticket at the KINE, opposite Jolly Lolly Yoghurt factory. I tell you, it was three deep, mile long, chock-a-block queue, so bad that if you suddenly got one of those scratch-or-die itches, you'd die for the want of scratch. At one point I thought, Make peace with your Maker, for any minute now you'll be catapulted across that street and plonked p-l-o-nk into one of those vats of strawberry yoghurt.

I won't even attempt to tell you what murder it was the rest of that day. Because I know it would touch off such depths of compassion in your christian heart, you'll just sob in sympathy with this poor old grumble bag, having to cope with this motley mob. But I must tell you what happened in the car park because it really shook me.

'Uuh, people!' cried the lady in the car parked next to mine, 'don't people ever work or sleep or do anything else but shop? All that t-e-eming mob at the KINE!' I then realised in a flash that since I was there I was part of that mob. Sheepishly I confessed, 'I was part of that mob, *your* mob.' Then we both burst out laughing. And as she drove off she mused, 'It's funny how you are *my* mob and I am *yours*. Makes you think, doesn't it?'

It does indeed.

My Fan-tastic Oh, Sole Mio

Ever laughed at your silliest madcap self? We did the other day, my Comic Imp and I. When I clicked on the goggle box and caught that bizarre Yea, Yea session, the Pop Shop.

'Yea,' mocked my Comic Imp, 'it's bizarre YEA, YEA now. But remember when you nearly went bizarre Yea, Yea yourself. Got that silly notion into your silly head that you can sing those soul-searing songs . . . like Oh, Sole Mio! Remember!

'That one day, 6.30 a.m: You in front of your bathroom mirror, mascara-ing your left eyelash: and the radio blaring Mario Lanza's Oh, Sole Mio! And how, in a click — you became maestro's competitor, remember? Stretching and screeching that MIO till you cried: Hooray! I got that crescendo higher than the maestro himself! Remember?

'And how for a spell, you went punch-drunk with your fame dream. Even used that fame and fortune potion whisky and honey — to make your voice mellifluous. Remember that? Sneaking to your bathroom with a tot of whisky and a pot of honey, then stirring that silly concoction with a toothbrush handle and then belting it out — between those millifluous sips — your masterpiece, Oh, Sole Mio!

'Mamma Mia! — that was a scream . . . that Sole Mio. then you adopted, remember that punkiest punk this side of loony bin, Boy George as your he/she hero, — and got hooked on his courage. Till you cried, ''The courage! To be now a hunky 'he' and now a dollied up 'she' — pigtails and all. The courage!'''

Then came one Yea, Yea session and my he/she Hero was dethroned in a click. 'What courage?' boomed my Comic Imp. 'Hiding behind those sunspecs, those glorified hidespecs. Hiding the shame of underserved fortunes. And the fear that any minute now that pigtail wig can slip off and reveal the truth — the egg-bald pate under it. You call that courage?

'You want to know what real courage is? The courage of the man in the street, of the millions of unsung heroes. Facing life's trials and tribulations, boring chores and daily dailiness. And still laughing with one eye, while crying with the other. That I call real courage.'

From then on my he/she Hero was dethroned forever and my rosy specs firmly stuck on. So that I can laugh with one eye, mostly at myself — while crying with the other!

Doppy Dopley on 'No Buzz' Strike

I chuckled myself silly while reading my American friend's letter about one private phone company. This was in the little village of Dopley (population 250), where people got so heartily sick of the sleepy telephone service that they decided to go on strike to beat all strikes — NO BUZZ Strike.

One week they notified all concerned, with an ad in the local paper, saying: Dopley is on a one week NO BUZZ Strike. Because we've had so many Sleepy Sallys for over twenty years now, that we decided what all our Sleepy Sallys need is one week of sound sleep — 168 hours!

And for a week, nobody in the village answered the phone. If they had an urgent message they sent it by a motorbike courier. They stuck to their 'no buzz' guns and, guess what, they have forced the telephone company out of their buzz business; and the new company is absolutely hoarse buzzing the buzzers and begging the subscribers to have fun with their new TeleFun. My friend is sending me a copy of their 'Have fun with TeleFun' pamphlet that she kept as a souvenir.

I can well imagine — can't you? — what it'll say: 'Have fun with our TeleFun! Our new service can bring you a new friend every time you pick up a phone — and get a wrong number. Because, that "wrong number" stranger is a potential friend you wouldn't have made if you didn't get that wrong number. So be positive! Strike a new TeleFun friendship every day!'

'Or you may be phoned by a total stranger who asks if you are a City Mortuary or somebody called Josiah Dillybumm. This will invariably result in them asking you if you are 923714 or some such. Now just think how much ice can be broken with a fun call like that. Particularly when it's late at night and you have time for a friendly chat. Fun friendship again — with your TeleFun!

'And of course you musn't forget all those crossed lines

— even more fun and friendship. When a third person can listen to your call. Two funbirds killed with one "hello"! Of course we can't guarantee a crossed line every time on every TeleFun line. But be assured our TeleFun technicians are working hard on getting as many crossed lines as possible.'

Just think of all the fun we are going to have when TeleFun comes your way — I can't wait!

Magic Of Electronics?
They Must Be Joking!

Uh, that bane of my life, the telphone! Sometimes I feel I could merrily empty a box of nicely rotten tomatoes at any of those electronic, sham-a-tronic telephone exchanges!

Because the way this electronic monster can fray my temper to tatters is quite UN-believable! Do you know, the other day I got through to Sydney, Australia in fifty nine seconds flat — I've timed it — fifty nine seconds, bell-clear, 60,000 miles away. And yet, an hour later I had a nightmare of a battle for over twenty minutes to get my friend's number (76358), less than six blocks away. Can you beat it? Twenty minutes, six blocks away!

And that was an SOS call at that. You see, that day I was looking after my friend's little boy and the little horror performed a major miracle — stuck his head, glove-tight, in a saucepan, right down to his nostrils. You can imagine the panic. Tried everything I could think of. Even had him lying down while I pulled the saucepan and my maid pulled his legs. But the wretched saucepan didn't want to budge — and that's it — not an inch.

That was a Do-It-Yourself horror show better than any ET.

Frantically I went on dialling for help. Dialled Ambulance, no reply. Dialled 76358 — boy's mother — twice and got ditto, no reply. Dialled Test-A-Number and got female squeaking, 'You must wait for your turn, in a queue, lady.' To which, like a looney let loose I screeched back, 'Wait?! I've got a saucepan in the head . . . I mean head in a suacepan . . . I mean child's head in a saucepan, suffocating and you want me to . . .' But the squeak didn't wait for my final screech. Just banged the receiver, bang!

Finally I tried 76358 again and at long last, hooray, I got it. But I only managed to say, 'Come Sue, quick,' when there was a beep-beep and the voice said, 'This is Post Office, testing your number. Please put down the receiver.

By that time I was beside myself. 'Holy saucepan,' I bellowed, 'Testing *my* number? It's not my number, it's my friend's number that wants testing.' Wherupon, you know what the electronic monster did? Went 3Ds on me. Dead, dead, dead.

A couple of nights after there was this programme on TV — you may have seen it — called *The Magic of Electronics*. All that bla,bla and tech gobbledygook you need three Einsteins to de-gook. All about esoteric codes and computer modes and a box of tricks called Autrax, that marvel of marvels that can transmit 50,000 telephone calls all over the world — that very one, I fancy, that couldn't get me one single number, six blocks away. It sure is a funny world.

Do-It-Yourself Valentine Card

Our Misery Mona (she of the 4000 moans) says: Can you believe it? I've just read somewhere that in America over six million Valentine cards have been sold this year. Six million! — and no doubt, millions more world-wide. And yet — would you believe it — I never got a teeniest, weeniest card ever. Nix, nil and none. Isn't this enough to make you cry?

It certainly makes me ready to cry into my vino, that very thought. And this year it's worse than ever. Every Joan and Jane I know seems to have got her Valentine card. But me. Even that creaky old Gran Gertie in the flat below. She got one from her grandson, with a PS and a kiss from Woofie, the hound. I tell you — it was a case of mental cruelty, just to hear her bragging about it!

And to beat it all, last night I click on my goggle box and what do I see? A preview of St Valentine's Day, with another love-crazed Valentino. You may have seen it. There he was, this romatic lovelorn, bless his bleeding heart — renting a plane, to trail, guess what? His great love message: JOHN loves JANET.

You can imagine how I felt. Devastated. My lonely heart just simply went sinking right down to my pink slippers. 'Renting a plane?' I cried, 'To trail a love message? And here is poor, unloved misery me, nobody's ever bothered to send me a plain little 'padded heart' card that wouldn't even have to be bleeding!'

It's a c-rr-uel world and that's for sure. But next Valentine Day, I have vowed now, there'll be no more bitter tears for me. No more crying into my goulash pot and my vino glass. Because, you know what I am going to do next year? I'll shame this cruel world and do myself a D.I.Y. Valentine. Just buy the biggest card, with a grotesque padded heart and four cherubs in four corners and across it I'll print my revolutionary love message: ME loves ME.

So see me next Valentine Day in front of my Valentine 'ME loves ME' card. And perhaps even — why not? — I'll pop a bottle of bubbly. To raise a toast to that great truth: That after all is said and all the tears are sobbed, love-like charity begins at home!

Those Mind-Boggling Manuals

This crazy world of ours gets crazier by the minute! Take all those mind bogglers called manuals for example. The way they multiply, we'll soon have a hi-tech manual, corrugated and stuffed into every box of matches, — giving you and me enough rubbish to start a rubbish recycling plant.

Take my latest candidate for *my* rubbish recycling plant. The manual for my new radio EXCELLA X 123 Twenty four pages of it and a truly mind-boggling bamboozler. Bragging on page *one* to have: One air damper button; one sound dampener knob; three hi-tech sound monitors; one anti-electric shock switch and even — don't faint' — one fire alarm button. The only gimmick button it hasn't got is a parachute to the Moon. And all of this, believe it or not — in seven languages. Including that Jap screed that looks like crazy scratchings of some intoxicated cockerel, deperately trying to prove it isn't, — intoxicated.

And that's page one only. Page two has an even longer list of jacks, knobs, and buttons. Phone jack, Input jack, Output jack, AC jack and seven other assorted jacks and buttons marked with all the letters of the alphabet — except Y. I suspect they were scared to put Y in case we ask *why* such a hi-tech mess.

I know what you'll think: Shame! Poor old fossilized fossil. She can't cope with all these ultramod, hi-tech concepts.

Well, maybe I can't. But my argument is: Can anybody? Know the difference between a jack, a switch, a knob, a button and a hi-lo mode monitor? I confess I don't. All the bamboozler is doing is making me wish I knew how to swear — in Japanese!

P.S. The above anti-bamboozle lament is only about three pages of the said bamboozler. I still have twenty one pages to scream about. In seven languages. The very

thought of ploughing through it leaves me out and out
speechless!

A Key Is A Tortuous Contraption

I don't know who invented it, but whoever did deserves a medieval torture of the most torturous kind. Who am I moaning about now? The inventor of that torturous contraption that's spelt K-E-Y, the key inventor, that's who.

And in this tirade I include my lifetime tormentor, my Macho Moustache. Because uh — that man and his nag, nag about how I always lose the keys! So right now — see me in the middle of my mop-mop session, my mascara drip-dripping, while I am inventing the most torturous torture a human mind can invent.

And you know what that would be? A medieval dungeon, but with a difference. The dungeon would have seventy seven doors and the prisoner would have a hefty bunch of keys, but not a single key would fit any of those seventy seven locks! And into that dungeon I'd throw all the other inventors, adaptors, locksmith fundis and all the yale lock monsters in the inventors' registrar.

And you know who would be the first prisoner on that devilishly clever motley crew list? My Macho Moustache.

Why him? Because he is forever creating un-merry hell about some keys or other. Niggle, niggle, niggle. And more niggle. You always lose keys! he niggles. Remember that Yale-key pantry door you banged shut, with a bunch of keys inside? And how you had to caterpillar yourself through that ten by ten ventilator? With me push-pushing you one eyebrow and half a leg at a time — remember? And how you chilled another bunch of keys in the fridge, next to the bottle of wine? and how, recently, we spent half a Sunday looking for the 'green label' bunch of keys and found them in a steamer. Being steamed nice and tender with your green Brussel sprouts — remember?

So now, my friend — now you know why Macho Moustache would also go to that dank dungeon. His crime being: forever telling me to remember what I forever want to forget!

But there is *one* thing I do want to remember and that's my inaugural speech at the Pearly Gates. When St Peter hands over that last bunch of keys to all those . . . heavenly mansions I was promised in heaven. Taram, taram and hear me thundering, 'Many thanks, St Peter, but no thanks. If there is one thing in this universe I *do not* want in my heaven it's . . . a bunch of keys, however heavenly!'

Money Is Da Monster!

Isn't is amazing what some people would like to be in the next world. One woman, for example — 44 size, four tyre waist and a couple of legs fit for a jumbo piano — wants to be . . . a fairy. And a man I know — a beanstring of a beanstalk — guess what he would love to be? A brassière. Belonging to Mae West, no doubt.

But back to the money monster. Now my Italian friend I call Mamma Mia because if she says ten words, seven of them would be 'Mamma Mia'.

Over a glass of vino Mamma Mia would say, 'St Peter had better LEESEN about dis next world BEEZENESS. Because, unless I get everthing free and gratis — jus' press a button and presto — and unless all money is ban, banish and abolish, I am not going to any next world — full stop, finito!

And before I could say, 'Me neither', Mamma Mia would singsong, 'As far as I am concern, St Peter can have all the next univarrs, con amorre — and all the brazziers! Because, Mamma Mia — Money is DA MONSTER!'

I agree — and what a monster! As soon as the first ray of sun hits my eye Da Monster is on the whip. 'Get up', it nags, 'Come on — up, up up. splitting headache? Don't feel like it? And all those uhs and ahs and ohs, again? Let me tell you there'll be no ahs and ohs. There'll be just one jumbo u-u-uh! When you have all those bills to pay and none of this monster to pay it with.'

'I am nagging?' the monster goes on, 'I like that! You are not doing badly yourself. In fact, I reckon you'd make a first class Nag Champ yourself. Nagging how you've to COUNT it and WATCH it and LOCK it and BANK it — and even SPEND it — how you ab-s-olutely SLAVE looking after this money monster.

'Some looking after — I do declare! Sticking money any old where, into any old teapot, flowerpot and bra. And what about that passion killer, your pantie girdle? And the time -remember?- when you stuck 200 greenbacks into that . . . passion killer (the pantie girdle) and flushed it — whoosh! — all down the loo. You call this looking after money?

'You poor old money martyr! You know — the trouble with you is that you want the lolly, but you don't want the labour. What YOU suffer from is that famous — ITIS called LOVE — HATE-itis. Not so?'

Sad to say — it is so.

My Darling Hubby's 'What Work?'

Men are funny creatures. Take my darling hubby for example. He for ever says, 'What work? You call standing over the shop counter, work?' And yet I feel sure that if he could step into my lazy shoes just for one day, he would jump out of them quicker than I can say 'shop'. Because, honestly, I do more work than any of those out-'n-out exploited slaves ever did in the Middle Ages.

For I never e-v-e-r- stop. From six in the morning till eleven at night. Three hundred and fifty days a year. The other fifteen days are my holidays and then THEY never stop. I mean my family — for ever wanting me to do things for them.

So in effect I never stop 365 days a year. From dawn to midnight. Two gulps of tea and I am in the kitchen, cooking breakfast for the family. With one hand turning bacon and the other mixing the porridge. With one leg in the kitchen and the other in the garden — like a cross between a juggler, a gymnast and a human yoyo. Seeing to the cat's milk and the dog's meat and the lunch box for the kids — the never ending list of 'ands'.

Or if it's not 'ands', it's musts and mustn'ts. Must remember the milk went sour, must connect the fridge, mustn't forget that broken plug or the char will electrocute herself. Must, must, must and quick, quick, quick — honestly the rush at that breakfast hour is something indescribable. I don't think even Willie the Bard could do it justice. When at last that rush hour is over, I am never in doubt whether I am coming or going. I know I am going round the bend.

So when eight o'clock comes and I am supposed to go to work and be as fresh as a dew-kissed daisy, I am often half-finito, long before the day has even began.

But off I whizz in my rickety Mini, my mind in a worry maze. Worrying: Have I connected back the fridge? Did I lock the store? And oh, dear, have I put away that broken plug or will I find the char stone dead on the kitchen floor when I come back?

Too late for that, I decide. The char must wait with her dying till I come back. And missing bikes, buses and telegraph poles — often by a hairbreadth — I now step into Bott's boutique.

There from 8.30 a.m. till 5 p.m. — nearly eight hours — I rarely sit; simply because there are no chairs to sit on. Mrs Bott, the manageress, doesn't believe in chairs. It's bad for business. She is the sort of creature who, if you complained your legs were dropping off, would say, 'Where?' A woman of fact she is. She'd want factual evidence.

I know my darling hubby would say, 'What about your lunch hour? Don't you get any rest then?'

During my break at lunch time I never stop either. There is always something to get from the shops. Like fresh fish or mended shoes to be collected. There is never a day without something to be done. So off I dash again — like a human jet — to be back in two ticks so that Maisie at the rattle counter can dash across the street to get her fresh fish. In fact, I often think with all this tearing hurry it's an out and out miracle that I haven't gone clean through that glass door at the fishmonger's — truly!

I can hear my darling hubby muttering, 'Come off it! You have plenty of time, all to yourself — after five!'

Well now — that's when my real work begins. Cooking supper and bathing the kids and seeing to their homework and seeing to hundreds of little chores. While my darling hubby l-e-i-surely pages through his paper and snorts, 'Work, what work? You call standing over a counter work?'

Men are funny creatures.

Have Fun With Your Phone, They Said

Our Misery Mona (she of the 4,000 moans) says: Just now, mark my word — my picture — complete with goofy teeth — will be in the next edition of WHO'S WHO (International), under T-Telephones, and next to the great immortal, Alexander Graham Bell.

And what's my claim to fame? My monumental discovery, that's what — and the biggest since A.G. Bell. So my friend, get curiouser and curiouser. Now, you know those phone hassles we all get: crossed lines and dead lines and hang-ons and those everlasting out of order fob-offs? Recently I have done some secret spying — (she-Sherlock Holmes style), and here is what I found: that all those phone pluggers at the exchanges are fibbing you when they say 'No reply' and 'Hang on' and 'Out of order', etc. They are just fobbing you off while they battle, poor things, with all those tangled up wires, all wriggling and screaming, like a giant can of worms, the whole wall of it. Small wonder, poor things, they can't cope!

And it's going from worse to worser with this newest craze for O-phones and Dial-A-phones. Dial-A-Joke and Dial-A-Tune and Dial-A-Prayer; and Car-O-Phones and Sky-O-Phones and Sex-O-Phones — hundreds of them. There is even Fun-O-Phone — (have-fun, -with-your phone) phone — can you believe it?

But the worst is what's all this jam-packing doing to God's good air. Soon it'll be so criss-crossed with decibels you won't be able to stick an Uh! Never mind 'Hello'.

I know all these high falutin -ists and -ologists will say, that peasized brain Misery Mona is the most ignorant ignoramus since God created a donkey. But to that I say I don't need to be an Einstein to figure it out that the air outside my house is not inexhaustible: and if you go on jam-jamming it with Joke-O-Phones and Sex-O-Phones you are bound to reach a point of exhaustipation. And that's what's happening, I phone my friend and get . . . City Mortuary.

But it looks as if, Lord be praised, the technologists are about to be out-teched and out-buzzed. Because, you know what's the latest buzz in the UK? Post Office is appointing official psychologists to deal with post office workers' stress. Good news for our poor hassled ears. I hope our post office workers get so stressed with Sex-O-Phones, they'll scream for shrinks. All we can do is hope it'll be soon. Or else we'll all be screaming for a national headshrinking service.

Whatever Next — A Preggy Papa?

I don't know about you girls and how you feel about Women's Lib, but I have a jumbo-size bone to pick with all these anti-lib gents — they make me m-a-d!

Like this hairy brute of mine, bless his rugby socks. Telling me Women's Lib is the joke of the century. After we have poured the cement down men's loos to get them to build women's loos; fought soda siphons to get into men's pubs; highjacked planes and robbed banks; after all that — and more — he has the cheek to say Women's Lib. is the joke of the century!

'But that's exactly what it is,' he argues, 'because, it's all very well for you libbers to cry, Hurray — we've become man's equal. Now we can even become welders and wrestlers and karate choppers. That's fine,' he says, 'But how long for? That's the point. How long can a woman stay a star footballer, for example? Till she gets married and gets pregnant and that's it. Psst goes her lib dream — like a pricked soap bubble.'

'Which means,' he concludes, 'that no matter how liberated you libbers become, there is one physiological function you can never escape. You'll always be females. You'll always be bearing our babies.'

Depressing, eh? To think that after all that welding and wrestling and karate chopping — not to mention the pinching of (male) bottoms — after all that, all we are fit for is rocking the cradle!

But we mustn't despair, girls. We mustn't just sit and mope, like a lot of feeble females. We must do something about it. And one thing we can do is to tell our scientists time they got cracking on this sex business. Time they stopped spying on flea's interior and cockroach's posterior and started engineering our innards a bit. After all, if they can produce wingless chicken, a square pea and a test tube baby, there is no reason why they can't make us all one

64

sex — unisex. All they have to do is do a little fiddle with a hormone or two, with a gene here and a chromosome there. So that eventually men can become equal to us and they too can bear babies and go 'halves' with us. So we'll have a preggy mamma this year and a preggy papa — producing triplets — the year after. A Compleat Unisex.

Impossible? If that's what you think, then I am sorry to tell you, you are displaying the most abysmal ignorance in matters scientific.

Because, did you know that the scientists have 'it-ed' that cool veg called cucumber? They have — it's a scientific fact. There used to be a 'he' cucumber and a 'she' cucumber; but now American scientists have invented a spray that makes an 'it' cucumber. One psst and that's it.

And that — I don't have to tell you — is only the beginning. Other pssts are sure to follow. Right down (or up) the biological tree. Till one day you and I will wake up to a TV announcer stunning the world, by saying, 'Dr Magdalena van de Merwe, a genetic engineering scientist, has invented the ultimate — a spray to end all sprays! One psst and your man can become a mamma.'

I was musing on these ideas, trying to work out where exactly are we going to be spraying all these darling brutes of ours — behind their cauliflower ears? — when my Comic Imp (the Great Debunker) whispered, 'That'll be the utterest of all utter ends! Can you imagine a man being preggy? Having morning sickness and having to go to work? And having to come back to three kids and a sick cat and the drains blocked? And having to cope with all that? Never! They'll all be commiting a mass harakiri, I am telling you!'

Poor us, slaves of Mother Nature. She always wins!

Help! I've Gone Click-o-Phobic!

All you young Einsteins clicking all these gadgets in two clicks flat — spare us poor oldies a tear or two! We really are in dire need of your sympathy. Because, honestly — all that modern click-click gadgetry is just about driving some of us oldies right up that proverbial wall.

Take my sad and sorry story. I tell you, you'll cry when you hear it. C-r-y for this poor oldie, enmeshed and entangled in the evil web of that modern monster called the washing machine.

Well now — you know that old rattlebox of a washtub? With one pump, one plug, one switch, the Pre-Year-Dot job with a mangle attached? I've had one of those for d-o-n-k-e-y's years. True, occasionally it would go on a blink, get duly fixed up and in between blink-outs I'd give it a hefty kick to its mechanical behind and whoopee! Nine times out of ten it would purr on like a charm, with no trouble at all.

Then a couple of weeks ago I won my first big prize in a competition. A magnificent mechanical beast: Supermatic, Superspin, SuperTwinTub — a perfect dream of a machine!

But that's exactly when my crying starts. Because you know what happened to that superdream of mine? Turned into a nightmare — in one single click. And all because — can you believe it? — all because I clicked the master switch ANTI-clockwise instead of clockwise and hell's bells — the bally monster shuddered and shook as if in a fit of mortal agony and well, just expired on me. Conked out, just like that — one click and kaput!

My husband says, 'What "kaput"? — that "kaput" can be fixed by a-n-y electrician in less than two clicks.' Maybe so, but — what *he* forgets, this Einstein of mine, is that I have another, much worse 'kaput' on my hands.

Like what?

Some sort of 'phobia, that's what. And much worse than

all the agro- and astro- and claustrophobias put together. I have contracted world's first click-o-phobia.

Fear of clicks. All of a sudden I am scared to death of anything that clicks. And just plain te-rr-i-fied of this click-click monster called washing machine.

I shudder to think what's going to happen next. When all these '-ists' and '-ologists' of the headshrinking ilk get to know about this rare mental aberration. They'll hound me, I can see it coming. Hound me like they do Boy George. With all those questions like, 'Have you ever eaten caviar with strawberry jam?' and 'What breed was your granma's shaggy mutt?' Can't you see the complications?

But of course, my dearly beloved can't see any of this. He says, 'Nonsense, study the manual, woman. Study the manual.' The m-a-n-ual? That, let me tell you, only gets me even more click-o-phobic. The moment I look at that drawing, with eighteen parts and thirty six arrows each going every which way; and with all those clicks and switches and hatches and even hangers — hangers, inside a washing machine, can you credit it? Can you blame me if I cry I need a travel guide and an Einstein IQ to sort out this little click-click lot!

And so — with tears in my eyes — I say, There it stands — my would-be pride and joy, still in its virginal state, not even christened with a drop of water. But I still insist that for the time being — a century or so — I am going to stick to my Pre-Year-Dot old beaut. All I have to do is get a new mangle. And with an occasional kick in its behind it'll last me twenty years or more.

I can hear my resident Einstein mutter in dismay, 'Get a mangle? — in this day and age? What you should do with this Pre-Year-Dot rattlebox is send it to the museum — with you as a principal exhibit: World's first click-o-phobic.'

Men, really. They are like machines, completely incomprehensible.

Me, Untidy? Never!

Have you heard about this latest cure for your pent-up emotions? In Japanese factories they have a special room full of the factory's big bosses, all of them life-size rubber dummies and every day between 10 and 11 a.m. any factory worker can go and do what he can never do in real life: give his boss a punch on his nose. They call these dummies very appropriately Punchie-kitos.

Right now I feel I could easily do with three of these Punchie-kitos of my family. Because, do you know what they did to me this morning? They vamoosed with my denture — would you believe it?! Two near adult youngsters and their father, the silly goat — playing silly tricks like that!

I was in my bathroom this morning when the telephone rang in the hall. So I quickly ran to answer it with my clean denture in my hand and of course, being in a hurry I must have left it — or at least I thought I did — on the telephone table. But when I went back to get it, it had gone! And — I later discovered — one left shoe of my black pair and a handbag to match. They too are gone. All part and parcel of the master plan to show me that I am not half as tidy as I profess to be.

This — I must tell you — has been a lifelong and forever losing battle over my family's untidiness. For years I've pleaded, I've reasoned, I've coaxed and cajoled and I even threatened, but all to no effect whatsoever. Till last Sunday it came to such a pitch that I decided, come what may, I have to issue an ultimatum. So I told them, One day there will be, Robbie the Robot who — with a click of your finger — will tidy all the mess that you leave behind. But until such time and from this moment on, anything that gets left where it shouldn't get left, gets thrown into the dustbin the very same day.

But — what do you think happened next? It boomeranged

on me, that's what. Before I could even execute my threat, they stole my thunder, they beat me to it. It was they in the end who picked all that *I* left where I shouldn't have left. Isn't it ironic?

And what's more — they couldn't have chosen a worse time either. Because in a few hours' time, I am supposed to be at the club and deliver a speech on 'Glamour for over Forties'. Glamour of all things! And here I am down in the dumps flop, without a peg in my head to bite my nails with! Really — life is too c-ruel for words!

And now for my postscript (three hours later), I don't know how to tell you this, but I have found my denture, guess where — in my dressing gown pocket. But I still can't go to that 'glam' do tonight. I have misplaced my car keys — I am still looking for them.

Those Unflappable Secretaries!

Our Misery Mona (she of the 4000 moans) says, Ever had to ring a boss and had to deal with that stoniest of all stone walls, the unflappable secretary? Then prick up your ears, my friend, there is a moan for you to share with my funny friend, Artemus Le Brusque a travelling agent who says, there ought to be International Rejection Week, dedicated to poor moaners like me who are rejected by secretaries who won't let them through to speak to their bosses. With some of those secretaries it's almost as bad as breaking the sound barrier!

Now Artemus (Artie for short) sells office pins and paper clips, wholesale, and reckons he must have sold a couple of tons of them, at least, over these twenty years or so — thanks to people's habit of fiddling with a paper clip.

Artie says, 'In my time, I have dealt with hundreds of secretaries and met all sorts. Including that funny creature who asks your name and if you say, John Smith, she'd say, Can you spell it for me? So you think, Spell John Smith? But still you spell it. S for Sam and M for Mike and I for Ivory. Wait a minute, she now says, what's Ivory? I got lost, she says. So you start all over again. S for Sam and M for Mike and I for Iron . . . By which time you lose your patience and sigh, U-u-uh! And she says, What's that U-uh for?

But most secretaries are efficient, intelligent and very obliging. They fall over their phones trying to help you. But there is that obnoxious one per cent of that secretarial sisternity — those un-flappable ones, and oh boy, can they obstruct you! And l-o-v-e doing it. You can almost hear them cry, Another human porcupine deflated!

Which is what I used to be. A human porcupine, b-r-i-s-t-l-ing with anger, every time I had to deal with those unflappables. They used to make me so flappable I'd be useless for the rest for the day, and half of the next.

70

Till I got tough and decided if she can invent all those devilish diversions, so can I. Two can play the same game. So now 'Kill a fib with a fib' is my strategy. If she says, 'Mr Bloggs has just gone outside' I say, 'He couldn't have. From this phone booth on the ground floor, that's facing the lift, I would have seen him, unless he flew like a Superman UP the lift shaft and through the roof. Do you think he could?'

Or if she says he is at a meeting, conference or seminar, I use another ploy: 'I am ringing from the sixteenth floor and through the window, I can see Mr Bloggs on the fourteenth sucking a toothpick after that caramel crunchy he had with his morning cuppa.'

But the best is my ALARM ALERT technique. If she asks what's my business, I cry, 'Fire!' or say, 'This is SPCA. The bulldog next door has savaged Mr Blogg's pet Persian, something cruel — one whisker is torn right off.' Now what can she do but let me through?

You might think I'd be unpopular with all secretaries. To the contrary, they *love* me, the good ones, when I pull down a peg or two those baddies that are 'good name' spoilers.

But most of all think of it this way: If I don't get through to her boss, I don't get an order, right? Which means I don't deliver, right? So Bloggs and Co. won't have any paper clips to fiddle with when they are telling all those fab fibs. See my point?

I told you, my friend Artemus is a very funny fellow.

The Gremlin And I

We all know about that bane of writer's life, the writer's block. But what about those pests called gremlins that so often plague our lives?

They always seem to appear just as you've overcome your longest and most hair-tearing writer's block. When you have finally completed that b-e-a-u-t of an article and feel so exhilarated you could literally kiss it — that's when the gremlins strike, dying to put a spoke into the wheel of your fame and fortune.

I know you will say, Gremlins, what gremlins? Now that I have my finished article what possible gremlins could there be now? All I have to do is put it in an envelope and post it.

Ha, ha, that's what you think.

Have you thought of your introductory slip and what will it be? Dear Sir or Dear Madam? Or maybe you decide neither. And put 'Dear Sir/ Madam/Ms' instead and proceed to type one concise sentence: 'I enclose my article entitled THE COCKROACH AND I and hope you can use it in your esteemed publication.'

Jubilantly you now cry, Done! And eagerly you pull out that sheet out of your typewriter. Only to find the gremlin-in-chief has done its dastardly deed. In utter horror you cry, Heavens, my carbon! I've put it the wrong way round. So that the editor would have got Dear Sir/Madam/ms in duplicate, back to back — on one sheet of paper!

But of course, being a dedicated scribbler, that's not going to stop you. Because you know that being a good writer means being a re-writer, *ad infinitum*, till you get it right. right? So you re-write.

At long last you sigh, I've got it! All I have to do is to put it all into an envelope and post it.

Ha, ha, that's what you think.

What you don't know is that at this very moment the

gremlins have gone into a little conspiratory huddle — yes, in that cobwebbed corner in your study — and *unisono* decreed, Operation MAJOR FOUL UP! And a dozen mistakes have been decreed to happen, exactly now. Between your introductory slip and your final 'licking the envelope' lip.

Such as?

Such as you find you put the wrong introductory slip — the one with your carbon on the other side, remember? (And unsigned):

Or you forget to put your stamp on your s.a.e.

Or forget the s.a.e. altogether.

Or you rmember the s.a.e but forget your masterpiece (THE COCKROACH AND I) and find it staring at you, just as you have given that envelope your last loving lick!

I know you will say, Come off it, you grumble bag — you need to be IQ 12 (when normal IQ is a 100), to make all these stupid mistakes with one envelope.

If that's what you think then I must be IQ 11 — for let me tearfully confess — in my 20 odd years of scribbling humour I have made them all, all these mistakes. And yes, sometimes three or four with one envelope!

My only consolation is that many a better scribbler than me has admitted they too have been plagued by those gremlins of all sorts and sizes.

What can you do about it? Somerset Maugham has the answer. Somewhere in his voluminous volumes he says: Have a good, fat laugh — and scribble on regardless!

Help, They Are Spying On Me!

There are some creatures on this earth that I will never understand — and that's scientists.

Because I mean, they have hundreds of subjects they could spy on. Like cockroach's whiskers and the sex life of a seahorse and which way round the bath water runs out, round or circularly. And scores of other subjects of equally monumental drivel. But who do they spy on instead? You and me.

I have done a spot of spying on these sleuths that spy on us and really, it's no joke. There is an army of them. Of all sorts of profs and docs and masters of science, all playing the funniest spy games you can imagine. Spying on just about on every mortal thing you do and every part of your anatomy.

And on oddest things ever. Like bumps on your head. Don't laugh, I am being serious. There are fellows called phrenologists, for example, who do nothing else all their lives but study the bumps — God given ones, I mean — on people's heads.

One such eminent 'bumpologist' boasts he has studied 18,000 human heads and has actually mapped them out. which bump is where and which bump means what — characterwise.

There are 'winkologists', sneaking around with micro-cameras in their tie pins, clicking pictures of your winks, trying to discover how many winks you wink per millisec when you are lying; and 'lipologists', studying the way you wear out your lipstick; and 'legologists' — the funniest breed of them all — who go snooping around in typing pools and offices, spying on your legs. For how you cross them and twist them and dangle them is sure indication how cross and twisted is your inner ego.

But the latest and the ultimate is 'dustbinology'. There is a man in America, by the name of William Ratje, an anthropologist, who says, Forget her kicks and licks and her head-bumps and winks, Just concentrate on her dustbin instead. Her dustbin, he declares, is *the* most reliable guide to her character.

My husband laughs, 'Whatever next? Hole-in-a-sock-ology? the science of holes in socks'. But to me it's no laughing matter. Because once all these -ologists know all my licks and kicks and bumps and winks, there won't be a scrap of secret 'me' left!

And what's the good of me, without that secret 'me' — tell me?

Uh, That Frankenstein Fraternity!

Everytime I say there is some Frankenstein Fraternity afoot, everybody laughs at me and says, 'Frankenstein Fraternity?' But I am telling you there must be some kind of universal conspiracy by the hooligans of the world to scare us, decent folk out of our wits and skins.

People can't see it, but I can. I can hear some Arch-Frankenstein booming on a laser beam from some cave in Outer Mongolia to all world's hooligans. 'Too many wets, wimps and weeds in this world! Kill them off! Or if you can't kill 'em scare 'em stiff!'

And that's exactly what they are doing. Because — look at the violence! It's murder a minute and no kidding. Do you know, the other day, I counted: five murders, three babies bashed, one sodomy, one jealous woman who bit her lover's ear right off, one man who bit a chunk out of his friend's nose because the friend swallowed his pet canary — alive — for a bet; and a sexy vixen who was luring her lovers into her boudoir, killing them and throwing the dismembered members to — a pool of crocodiles — all this in *one* paper!

By Saturday that week — I shouldn't wonder — the scaremongers had a ball. Embroidering all this gory ear, nose and limb lot and crowning it with a gruesome finale, like: *Sexy vixen wants dentures for her crocsy croc*!

No wonder we all sh-sh-ake and sh-sh-iver and lock, lock, lock and stuff, stuff any measly dime and cent into our anti-static knickers — no wonder!

But it's my Comic Imp, the resident jester inside me, that has the last prophetic word. 'That's nothing,' he whispered, 'Wait till the news comes via satellite from all seventy seven corners of the earth. When they won't be just reporting murders. They'll be *announcing* them. Giving you and me a kind of pre-view of pre-murder. So instead of shaking and shivering, you'll just click on you TV and drop dead gedung!'

'And let me tell you — this Frankenstein Fraternity is already in cahoots with undertakers. Because — have you heard the latest in coffins? They are going to be cardboard and foldable. To bury the dead standing. No wonder — if they are going to scare us all into so many instant stiffs, there won't be any room for lying in comfort, horizontally. What a world to live in!

Down With Holidayitis!

Have you heard of that mysterious disease called holidayitis? The experts define it as that crazy craving for a holiday — having just come back from a holiday.

When I told my husband how clapped and *finito* I felt, he wasn't a bit amused. 'Three days after three weeks' holiday,' he cried, 'and you crave *another* holiday? You must be joking!

He then gave me the usual, oh-so-loving lecture. On what's wrong with me. 'What's wrong with you is,' he said, 'that you never plan your holidays. It's all one big helter-skelter. You never give it a thought — not even as near as three weeks before. Three days before you *might* start thinking: I must start thinking. Then on the day of going and thirty minutes before we start, you start. And boy oh boy — it's as if a hurricane hit the house. You pull all the drawers out and you stuff, stuff, stuff all the suitcases any old how with any old thing. What you need is to learn how to plan your holiday, plan your wardrobe, plan your luggage, plan everything.'

That of course is so much male chauvinistic tripe. I let you judge. Because let me tell you, if there is one thing I do well is plan. You should see some of those plans — immortalised on my cigarette boxes. They are masterpieces, every one of them.

So it's not that I don't plan. It's what happens to my plans after I've planned them.

And what happens to those plans? you ask. They disappear, that's what happens. I'd have the most minutely detailed plan for packing into one suitcase all that went into four before; or I'd get a brainwave how to build a wardrobe of four tops to match one pair of slacks. And I'd get it all down — oh, so neatly on my cigarette box. Only to find by the time I reach for another cigarette, my box is gone and my master plan with it.

Last holiday I spent hours planning my perfect wardrobe around one colour: brown. All I took with me was one short skirt, brown, one pair of slacks, ditto, four tops to match and only one pair of shoes to go with them all.

But guess what happened the very first night as I was dressing for dinner and cabaret? That jolly heel came off. No wobble, no warning — just like that, just took and came off. So I could either hobble on one brown heel or wear my beach tackies, dirty denim blue. Instead I had a stiff enough whisky to drown all my holiday flops and fiascoes.

But this year I am going to have the best planned holiday ever. In bed. I know you are going to say: 'But you can't stay in bed for three weeks, not being sick!'

You want to bet? I've got it all planned already. On my cigarette box, of course.

All You Can Do Is Laugh

Don't you think we ought to have some kind of Mums-of-the-World-Unite! Because all our lives we slog and slave to bring up our children but no sooner we bring them up, they are away and gone. I really do think a mum is the most exploited creature on earth. For where is the institution that would leave you as empty-handed — and sore-hearted — as Mother Nature does? After twenty years of hard love-labour?

Poor me, the mum in question and pa (my worse half) have just gone through the most gruelling experience. Our daughter Tracy has just left home to fend for herself. Just like that. One day she was with us and the next day she was gone.

One day I was stirring my stew in the kitchen, when in walks my little Tracy back from the office, all jumping for joy. 'Mum, guess what,' she cried, 'Norma, my friend, has asked me to share a flat with her. Don't you think it's fabulous?'

Fabulous? To me it was anything but. I was shattered. I did put on a brave face but inside me I was like a weepy willow, all the time swallowing the invisible tears. I couldn't believe it was happening to me. My *baby* leaving home, for good, forever. It can't be, I thought, it just can't be true.

But it was. That night I didn't sleep a wink. I tossed and I turned and I kept on lying down and getting up — like a neurotic yo-yo. One side of me sobbing, 'She is too young at 18!' and the other side sobering me up. 'You can't cling to her forever. You can't hold the clock back.' While pa, guess what — was snoring his nostrils out. And snorting between snores, 'I'll never understand you. For years you blubber and bluster what a headache she is and how you can't wait to see her go and now that she is going, you are crying your eyes out!'

But the night she left was even worse. I don't ever want

to live through another one like it. I didn't even bother to get undressed. Aimlessly I walked from one corner of the house to another, re-living happy memories and re-hashing unhappy regrets. Minutes seemed hours and hours stretched into eternity; while I kept hoping and praying she ring and say, 'I am lost without you. Please come and fetch me home.'

But the phone remained tomb-dead silent.

Then around lunch time next day it rang — and it was Tracy. My heart skipped a beat. At long last, I thought. My baby is homesick, she's missing me.

But she wasn't. Because her first words were — guess what — 'How is Sooty, my daarling cat?' Can you believe it? Not a word about ma and pa and how she was missing us — only about her 'daarling cat!'

And she was quite upset when I told her the cat was all right. 'What do you mean all right?' cried Tracy. 'Doesn't she miss me?' 'Yes,' I joked, 'terribly. In fact, she is writing you a love letter with her loving paw, right now.'

'Stop joking,' cried my darling, 'I was worried about her. She must be going round the bend without me.'

She then caught herself, mid-thought. 'Oh, Mum!' she cried. 'Don't misunderstand me. Don't think I wasn't thinking about you, or thinking more about Sooty than you. Because I was. Thinking more of Sooty. I mean of you. I mean . . . Oh, you know what I mean! It's only that Sooty's a dumb creature and can't cry like you. And it helps if you can cry sometimes — you told me that yourself.'

I put down the receiver thinking, I hope she remembers that other great maxim: that it helps to live through your sad moment of life if you can find laughter even in your tears.

The Martyr Of Spit And Polish

You really get so shaken reading newspapers nowadays. Take this poor man who divorced his wife because she made him — wait for it — polish the soles of slippers religiously, every day — for thirty nine years! Can you believe it? the august judge was aghast. 'That makes,' he gasped, '733 soles polished a year. Multiply that by forty — and . . . Great Scott . . .'

Great Scott: And what a great lesson for us all and for me in particular.

'You can say that again!' mocked my Comic Imp. 'You weren't just houseproud, my friend, you were gone right round the bend, bonkers, houseproud. Remember that kist? Boy, wasn't that a laugh and a half?'

Remember? How can I ever forget? That antique dust trap! Made out of heavy teak wood, a magnificent master piece, beatifully carved all over with monster dragons and each with a monster dragon's eye. No, no eyelashes, thank goodness. But oh, I tell you, I got so hooked on those dragon's eyes that eventually — please don't laugh — I had to have set of toothbrushes to polish those . . . beloved dragon's eyes!

But what shook me off that 'hook' was a bout of flu I had. I remember sitting bolt upright in bed, sneezing my nose out and crying, 'My kist, my kist! I've never dusted it for . . . two days!'

'And two hours and twenty two minutes,' merrily mocked my Comic Imp. 'Imagine it! Poor dragon's eye, feeling s-o unloved! Go on — crawl out of your bed on all fours, now, and have your toothbrush love session with your beloved dragon's eye — now!'

I sneezed a hoot of a laugh into my tissue while my Comic Imp mocked on. 'or else you'll miss the crown. And the glory. At the Pearly Gates one day. You'll miss St Peter declaring, Welcome to the Martyr of the Spit and Polish.

To be known from know on — and for all eternity — as St. Toothbrush the Proud.'

You can well guess the rest. I crawled out of that bed and I hit and kicked that dragon's eye till my both feet hurt. I then phoned Mac, the auctioneer. 'Mac,' I croaked, 'I want to kick out of my life a monster. A dragon's eye. Come and get it. Sell it, give it away, whatever, I don't care — just take it away.' Poor Mac must have thought I've gone bonkers and looney.

But now, years after, you know what, I still sometimes wonder who's kissing him/her/ it now. I mean my dragon's eye. With a tootbrush, like I did. Lovingly.

3

SHAMPOO AND SET

Shampoo And Set — And Allied Tortures

Men, really, don't you think they have a peculiar sense of humour? Take my hubby for example. Every time I come back from my hair-do at Jeannie's my darling brute says, 'Enjoyed yourself?' After all that head-drenching and hair-tearing (literally by the roots) he is asking me if I enjoyed myself!

Enjoyed myself, indeed! Right now I feel the time has come for me to tell all those ignorant males of this world who exactly does enjoy this un-joyful happening called shampoo and set.

In my case Gentle Jeannie does. That's who.

She is the chief hair-puller in this hair-tearing (literally by the roots) establishment. You should see her when she gets me into that little cubicle of water tortures — boy, oh boy, does she love it! Once my head is bent over that sink my Gentle Jeannie is dead to the world — enraptured in scratching. Kneading my poor scalp and working up foam, and scratching.

And it's no use complaining that the water is boiling hot, for all she will do is turn on another tap — freezing cold — and scratch on regardless. Or slap a dollop of even colder cream and start all over again. Till the water is in my eyes, my nose and down my neck. and when at last I lift my head and cry, 'You nearly drowned me!' all she says is 'No extra charge for drowning, Madam,' and grins. Adding *sotto voce*, 'last seat in the far corner, please.'

By now, I tell you, I feel exactly the way I look — like a sewer rat. But worse is yet to come. For now Miss Joy wiggles her sexy derrière onto the scene. And if Jeannie is top hair-puller, Miss Joy is a champ.

I have watched her many times and truly, she is a she-robot. Pulling and pricking and rolling those rollers as a robot would roll a row of Swiss rolls. Throughout it she never smiles — except when I 'ouch!' And when I do she says to Sally, her assistant, 'Large curler with big spikes, please.' Then she ends it all in a grande finale. 'Put her under,' she says and vanishes.

Now down comes the drier, S-L-A-M! And now I am truly entrapped and encapsulated, worse than an astronaut. For the next twenty minutes I can't read or write, talk or drink or even sneeze without the monster (too hot, too cold, too high, too low), getting in my way. So that when I am finally freed and Joy is full of the joys of (hair) spring, all I want to do is run, f-a-s-t!

Next time darling brute says, 'Enjoyed yourself?' I am going to send him for a shampoo and set — never mind he has only three-and-a-half hairs in five rows. Then joy, oh joy — I can ask him for a change, 'Enjoyed yourself darling?'

Miss Succulent Sausage

Uuh, this cruel world of ours — truly! Take for instance all these beauty contests and all that jazz. It's all s-o unfair! Because just think: there's a beauty queen born every minute and a Miss Something or Other every other minute. Like Miss Egg Unbeatable and Miss Kosher Toothpaste and Miss Hungry Goulash — all jetset celebrities. And here is poor little me, honestly — I could weep! I am not even a princess of a piffling little sausage, with all my talents.

You may laugh, but it's not a laughing matter. Because, what am I going to do at the Pearly Gates when St Peter asks me, 'Been queen?' And all I'd be able to say is 'Nope. Been queen of Nix and Nil and Nothing.'

Makes me feel such a flat-footed flop. So bad, that last time when they crowned Miss Hot Paprika at the local hyper, my inner rebel read out the riot act, loud and clear: 'Enough is enough! Of all this 'forever flop' self-image! From now on it's all DO and DARE. like Miss Hot Paprika did — and dared. Seen how she stuck red hot peppers in her ears — without batting an eyelid? And won her crown — naturally. He who dares wins. So go on, dare. Go for a sizzling title, like Miss SUCCULENT SAUSAGE, and an exotic gear, like a hoola-hoola skirt. And I bet you'll win — and stun this crr-uel world!'

For days in my mind's eye, I could see the glory of it all. me on a throne, and me in a crown, and me in a hoola-hoola. with a string of succulent sausages round my neck, and all the world's cameras click-clicking this seventeenth wonder of the world! All I needed now was a sponsor — some artistic butcher wanting to promote his sausages à la hoola-hoola.

But guess who sabotaged my dreams of stardom? My dearly beloved — as usual. When I told him I am going to be Miss Succulent Sausage and even had an artistic butcher for a sponsor — my dearly beloved nearly had a cadenza!

'If you think,' he perorated, 'that I am going to be MISTER Succulent Sausage and watch you g-rr-unch that crunchy crown — dolloped thick with marge de luxe — like Anneline Kriel does; and have all these press pests spying on you every time you sniff and sneeze — you've got another thing coming . . . and that's divorce!

So once again, bang goes another of my dreams of stardom. But never say never, that's my motto. With my four spare tyres round my midriff, who knows — I might yet be crowned . . . Miss Michelin Tyre!

At Last — Eyelashes For Men!

Don't you think this funny world of ours is getting funnier and funnier by the minute? With all this itch-itch for change and all this crazy craving for new fads and new fashions that seem to go out almost before they even come in.

Sometimes I wonder how I survive it all — and smile — really. Because I mean, everybody is just i-tch-ing to change this poor yours truly. Change your dental floss, they say, it'll change your life; and change to Tizz-Tizz fruit salts, it'll change your ego; and change to something else and it'll change everything else — and stop your snoring. And when I tell them, 'But I don't snore.' They say, 'Never mind, it'll stop you getting mad when your husband snores.'

Can you beat it! It's enough to make you a nervous wreck and go gaga, isn't it? Like that woman I read in a paper recently. Poor thing, every time she hears 'change' her left eyelash goes blink-blink and her right nostril goes on a twitch-twitch like a rat's whisker!

I haven't a blink or a twitch yet — but it's coming the way things are going — definitely. I can see I'll be sprouting nervous whiskers, never mind twitch-twitching, just coping with all those changoholics. Or what my Italian friend calls — even better — let-a-loose changoholics.

There is, I tell you — an army of them. All sorts of fashion fundis forever playing all those funny yo-yo games with my hem, for example. I never know where my hem is going to yo-yo next — down to my ankles or up to my knobbly knees!

Or take that other yo-yo perennial they all just love playing: What's IN and what's OUT game. Like one season they would decree, Waspy waist is in. Waspy waist for me? Waist 40 plus — and hiding between two cellulite tyres? Have a heart, really. And then — the heartless lot — they would bring in h-u-ge baseball shoulders, to match those waspy waists. Now I ask you, can you imagine what I would look like, five feet nothing with a baseball shoulder? Like a she-miniature Bowzer!

But their latest is still the funniest. Because guess what they want to do next? Don't faint — redesign my face. I tell you, I took one look at this futuristic me-engineering and my chin dropped to my wishbone — and kept d-r-o-pping. I couldn't believe it! Redesign my face? Widen my cheeks and re-shape my eyes and re-mould my chin and one beauty boffin-bright spark wants me to restructure and beautify my perky nose with a moondust nostril blusher — moondust of all things! Whatever next will they dream up for me? A Yul Brynner no-hair hairstyle? With a plastic rose on top?

But whenever I get into this 'What's the world coming to' mood, my Comic Imp inside me steps in to cheer me up. 'Cheer up,' it said as I was paging through the glossie, 'and see the funny side of it all. Look what's coming to our poor macho men, for example. The Peacock Era, that's what's coming. Then they'll be wearing velvet suits in jewel colours and sparkling earrings and plastic beards and even believe it or not — stick-on eyelashes!

'Which means, can't you see?' my Comic Imp chuckled on, 'that at long last you'll be able to say to your dearly beloved: "For mercy sake, stop fiddling with that gipsy earring and stop fishing for that lost eyelash. Just jolly well glue on another pair. We are already twenty minutes late!"'

Boy, oh boy — what a joy that would be. It sure is a funny world!

Who, Me, Hypochondriac?

I am fed up, I told my friend Nelly, fed up to my teeth with all that cheer-up pep-up talk of hers. All she ever says is, 'Common, cheer up! Stop looking like a droopy drip and start looking for the funny side of life. You'll be amazed how quickly you'll perk-up!'

Perk-up indeed — the very thought is enough to make me feel like two droopy drips. Because what is there to be so chirpy and cheerful about — for me anyway? It's all very well for *her* to talk. She hasn't got *my* problem. I grant you, she has this sugar diabetes and she does get her bad turns and comas, but what's that nowadays with all the modern drugs? A jab or two and she is as sprightly as a flea in a circus.

Not like this poor little me here with my conjunctivitus and something else-itus and all the other-ituses. No wonder I always ache all over like a pin cushion. Only have to think 'Head' and I've got a headache. And my pain also is peculiar, to say the least of it. It travels, do you know that? From head to foot and from limb to joint. As if I had some mobile bughouse inside me, with the bugs now biting here and now biting there. But when I tell Nelly this she thinks it's a great joke. 'Must be,' she says, 'when the bugs get fed-up with your head that they move to your toes.' Ha, ha, very funny!

And what about my chronic — and rare nail condition? She forgets that. That's another thing, you see. She is so besotted with her sugar levels and insulin and diabetes, she completely forgets that my nails are shot, absolutely shot. You should see them. They are so brittle they break in pieces. And peel. You can actually peel my nails like you can peel a parboiled potato.

But what am I doing about it? You ask. Spending a fortune on it. That's what I am doing. On nail creams and calcium pills, all imported from America. Till I am ready to pop with pills. And where does it get me?

Nowhere. And it's now moving to my toenails. My left big toe is gone already — cracked — when I kicked that bicycle last weekend. But what does Nelly say to that? 'What do you expect,' she says, 'when you kick your toe like it was a horse's hoof!' That's your sympathy for you.

And what's more — it's going to get worse, the doctor says. He says my hair will fall out and my eyebrows *and* probably my eyelashes. Which will go first, left or right — I mean eyelashes — I don't know. But imagine it! What a prospect to look forward to. With one of my eyebrows maybe bald and the other half moth-eaten and without eyelashes — I mean I'll look like a cross between and albino and a Chinky man!

But I know exactly what's going to happen when Nelly goes to hospital for her next coma check-up and when I go to visit her. I know what she is going to say the moment I mention my poor nails. I can bet my last calci-pill she'll be chirping again: Come on, cheer-up and come on, perk-up! Look at the funny side of it all!

Funny side indeed — really, some people!

I Was An Appro Addict

Have you ever, my friend, stood well aside from yourself and looked at the funny self you once used to be? When you chuckle and cry in utter disbelief, could that really have been me? Was I really like that?

I tell you, on that subject alone I could chuckle all day long, even now years after. And write a book as thick as a telephone book all about those funny 'me' of times gone past.

When I used to be a PERFECTIONIST — particularly about my clothes. If one pleat in one place on a goray skirt was slightly askew, I'd press and re-press that pleat and look for more skews till there were no straights or skews left — just one big mess.

Or if the buttons on a dress didn't match that tiny little purple speck — but perfectly — I'd hunt and wangle an appro — yes, a button appro, believe it or not — then go right round the button bend: because, need I tell you, if the colour was right, the size was wrong and if the colour and size were right, the shape was wrong. Imagine — what a way to go round the beauty bend!

Those were those funny 'me' days. When I used to be a certified appro addict. Spending half a day hunting for an appro and two nights after fitting them on. And shoes, I mustn't forget those. Since the shops would only give you one shoe on appro, I'd get four left shoes and then, guees what — hold my grand 'hobble on one shoe' fashion parade. Can you beat it?

And belts — that used to be another perfect nightmare. I remember one tatty old skirt that I took to my silly head to rejuvenate with a fancy pink belt I saw in a glossy magazine. And what a battle of the belts that was! Mixing up all the belts and all the packets and all the appro dockets. Till in the end it was like fighting five pink snakes in the middle of the night!

95

But what finally took the appro cake was one pillbox red artificial rose that I wanted to match with the pillbox red tulip design on my black chiffon dress. Needless to say, all the roses I took on appro never came anywhere near that particular pillbox red. Whereupon — guess who rescued me from the jaws of the demon of perfection? My husband. With a smirk on his face and a grin from ear to ear, my darling brute said, 'I tell you what, I'll put you out of your misery and paint you a pillbox red rose right onto your chiffon dress. I've got a little of that pillbox red paint left over from that dustbin lid I painted — remember?

And what's my addiction now? you ask. Laughing at myself, at that funny 'me' of the days gone by.

Help! They Are Pinching My Bubbles!

Here is a chuckle about cheating I am sure you'll enjoy. About this American chatting on the radio about the cheating that's going on in America. Everybody's cheating, he says. Publicly and privately. Some even play a double cheating game. They brag to friends how rich they are and to the taxman how poor they are — in the same breath. If truth had to be told, there would be 200 million Americans in court — all defended by Perry Mason.

It starts you thinking, and adding up. All those pinching games the cheats are playing. With your sausage rolls and your flex on the radio and your toilet roll sheets and your tags and your matches — the list is endless. Even holes on your belt they pinch — no kidding. There used to be five holes on my belt, but my last belt has only three. Two holes less obviously pinched. But what can you do? You can't go and accuse them of pinching two holes out of your belt, can you?

Or take that proverbial cherry on top of your cake. It used to be a whole cherry. Now you are lucky if you get a quarter. the other day I only got a *hole* where the cherry was, honest. Soon we won't talk about the cherry on top. It'll be a 'cherry hole' on top!

And if such wide-spread cheater-choppery goes on how much goes on secretly that we don't even suspect? I mean, what's to stop them pinching a hundred grams of rice out your bag, as an example. If they sell millions of rice bags? They'll have another quarter of a million bags free — won't they?

Far fetched? I'll prove it to you it isn't. Because you know what I've discovered? They are pinching my bubble out of my bubblebath. Don't laugh. I mean it. My last sachet was at least a hundred bubbles short, obviously pinched. Because my bubblebath used to be a Nirvana dream, a Mount Everest of bubbles and with me in it all you could

97

see was my perky nose above it. But now it hardly covers my big toe — all right, my two big toes — even when it's 'bubbled up.'

I was relaxing in this bubbleless bubble bath, reflecting on this cheater-pinchery that goes on, when my Comic Imp suddenly chuckled, 'You had better stop moaning about your bubbles being pinched. Because, you know what, just now they'll have a Bubble Control Ministry with an army of Bubble Control ministers; And once they'll start nosing into your bubble affairs, you don't know what cheatery they'll dig up. Yes, Yours!'

Oh, For A Fig Leaf!

Everybody has some *cri de coeur*, something he must get off his chest come hell or high water. Right now my *cri de coeur* is: Why oh why doesn't some designer design a fig leaf to cover me from nose to knees? So that I wouldn't have to try thirty seven dresses that *don't* fit to get one that fits.

'Shake hands,' you say. And I say, 'That's good, because I know you'll understand what I mean. My sigh for a fig leaf is yours too.'

With me it's the same every season. New season comes and I go dress hunting, — in my lunch hour, of course — trudging from shop to shop, trying and fitting only to find nothing fits.

Not a thing. Like last week, when I spent four of my precious lunch hours trying dresses. Went to eight shops and tried thirty seven dresses, with thirty seven zips to zip and zip down — imagine it. Not to mention those loop buttons that loop and don't button. When the assistant in the last shop offered me a cuppa, I snapped, 'A double whiskey more likely!' and I stormed out of the shop.

It was an ordeal, I tell you. I went through all the 9s, 10s, 10½s, 11s and 87s — the lot. But all of them were just one big maze of mis-sized. Some 9s were miles too big and yet 11s-the *bigger* size — were skintight; and the one in between, 10½, could have accommodated two of me — when I was preggy and eight months gone!

Crazy, isn't it? All of which adds up to my plea, which most people will support: Why don't they standardize our sizes?

Now, I know for a fact that every season the manufacturers hold a Colour Council to decide what colours will be in fashion for the coming season. Why not have a Size Council? Why don't they get together and make up their minds what size is 34, 9, 10, 10½, 11 or 87?

Of course their defence will be: That's impossible. The human figure has always defied definition; there are too many variables. But we say: Nonsense. Particularly in this day and age when you can put a transistor on the head of a pin.

I am no designer, nor am I a pattern maker, so I wouldn't presume to teach a pattern maker how to make patterns. But I do know they could start by discarding all those antiquated 10½s and 11¾s that went out with the Victorian bustle. And then design a number of standard patterns that would be regulation for all makes. At least we could then hope that one in ten dresses would fit, instead of one in thirty seven.

Then poor little me could at long last stop sighing, Oh, for a fig leaf to cover me from nose to knees!

My Battle Of The Bulge

If you want to stay happily married, there is one thing you must never do. Never ask your husband, 'Darling, how do you like this dress?' Take my dearly beloved. Usually he doesn't notice a thing about what I am wearing. I could be wearing a fur coat in a blazing sun, he wouldn't notice it. But the moment I ask? 'Darling, how do you like this dress' he'll find enough faults with it for me to want to shred it with the garden shears!

So over the years I've learnt my lesson: I don't ask him. I just wear what I like — Whether he likes it or not. But now and again this little mortal me gives in to that oh, so human vice — vanity — and I *do* ask him.

Like with this cocktail dress I had bought for a special occasion. It was scarlet red, it was chiffon, had a black rose for a touch of drama, it was simply te-rri-fic! I just *had* to ask him.

And all I got was, 'H-mm, not bad.'

'Not bad?' I cried. 'A dream of a dress and all you can mumble: Not bad? What's wrong with it, anyway?'

'It bulges,' said my beloved, bluntly. Then he quickly corrected himself — for the worse — 'it's not the dress that bulges. It's you who bulges.'

'Me bulge?' I barked back. 'I suppose you'll now find twenty bulges?'

His reply was that he didn't say twenty or even two — 'But,' he went on, 'if you want to torture yourself have all twenty — and a couple of Michelin tyres thrown in, for good measure!'

After that lesson in higher maths I got myself a corselette. talk about medieval tortures! I had to wriggle myself into it as if I were a caterpillar on two legs. But when I slipped my dress on again my husband was delighted. 'Look at that figure — as good as any Miss SA!'

But, alas — the thrill only lasted precisely three and a half steps. Or as long as it took me to walk from where I stood to where I sat, at my dressing table. Simply because I couldn't stand up when I sat down. I couldn't even breathe, never mind talk or laugh. I felt as if I was squashed in a vice. I simply had to take it off — and quick!

So I didn't wear that medieval contraption to the party. But I never asked my husband, 'Oh, but darling, — can't I go *without* that corselette?' I just went without it — Michelin tyres and all.

And the compliments I got! Yes, from him. All about what a wow of a figure I had in that dream of a dress!

'Must have been that medieval armour!' I joked. Thinking to myself, At long last I've learnt my lesson. Never to ask HIM how he likes what I am wearing. Just wear it.

Time To Cry — Over Yourself

Oh my dear friend, spare me a tear or two — I feel so miserable! I have just sprung this great big granma of a boil and it's grow-grow-growing on the left side of my nose. I look like a well-pickled alkie with this red bulb of a nose. Can't smell, can't sniff, can't even sneeze. All I can do is snivel-plain terrible!

But do you think anybody cares? Not a sausage of soul. Can you believe it?! Great big granma boil staring at them — spit in the eye — and as big as *two* noses on my left side, and nobody has even murmered, 'You, poor you!'

Not even my dearly beloved. All he does is lovey-dovey with his perishing Persian Perky. 'Poor little Perky!' I heard him cry, 'Poor litle Perky, your whisker is going so grey!' I ask you.

And that got me so fuming mad I gave the door three mega kicks and ran for my little *tête à moi* retreat, in front of my bathroom mirror. And of course, you know who was there — my Comic Imp — the pest!

'What's all this snivel-snivel about?' he asked. 'Your nose? Nobody wants to snivel with you. Not even your dearly beloved! But there is a very good reason for that, so be prepared for a shock. He too has a boil. A carbuncle in fact, with a plaster all over it. Haven't you noticed it? Great big granpa job.'

'Oh, yea,' I snivelled back, 'you want me to believe that?'

'Believe it or not, he has. He is going to have it lanced this morning. And you haven't even noticed it!'

I held my snivel — and my breath while my Comic Imp went on with his bitter-sweet lecture. 'So we have now this . . . grand snivel drama. *You* have two noses on the left side and half a nose on the right, and he has the same, only in reverse. Maybe we could, sort of . . . between the two of you, make one good nose out of half of his and half of yours.'

'Good heavens! Comic Imp!' I cried. 'Things you invent to make me cry!'

'I have to,' chuckled my Comic Imp, 'invent things to make you *think*. Make you realise that number one fact of life: That the world, alas, does not turn around your nose, or for that matter around his.'

Then the rascal gave me his usual parting shot. 'But you must give me that much. I do make you laugh — at least with one eye — while you cry with the other!'

Progress And My Poor Pet Piggy

Our Misery Mona (she of the 4,000 moans) says, I have a friend living on a smallholding near Knysna and she moans:

I am so distressed, I have just lost my pet piggy Clarissa and under the most extraordinary circumstances. It all started a while ago when the morning paper carried the following headlines: 'New Victory on the B.O. Battlefront — deodorant for pigs'. The paper went on to say that a local firm had actually gone into production for the next pig-sweating season. Which was followed by a news item from America where a progressive farmer was reported to be laying wall-to-wall carpeting and installing showers in his Iowa piggeries.

My first reaction was, whatever next? Slumberland for pigs? But then I thought I mustn't be old fashioned and stay in the way of progress for pigs. Why not instead introduce my pet to some hazards of civilisation? Give her a shampoo or two and a whiff of deodorant, so that she'll be better conditioned to the coming changes.

So that's what I did. But oh — what a fiasco! Starting with my deodorant I grabbed Clarissa by her front trotter and gave her a whiff of my Beauty de Luxe. You should have heard her squealing! As if I was going to chop the jolly trotter off and make a jelly out of it — there and then. And the shampooing was even worse. She just did not want to be shampooed. She squealed loud enough for ten pigs and then, free of her tormentor — me — she trotted off for a lovely wallow in the dirt and remained there for hours! Next morning, terrified of scent, soap and me, she gave a couple of snorts and pronto bolted into the wilds, back to Mother Nature. Poor pet, she has been lost for over a week, without food or water — and for all I know, she may even have been guzzled up by some greedy guts in the wilds of the Knysna forest.

You can well imagine what I could do to all those

progress-mad 'with-its'! Meanwhile, being a passionate pig lover, I feel duty bound to warn this progress-mad world. Somebody's making a grave mistake with all this de-pong the pigs business. Because it's all very well for the 'with-its' to say , 'We'll de-pong the pigs' — but have they asked the pigs if they want to be de-ponged?

My pet Clarissa most certainly doesn't. And if this is the general feeling in the world's pigdom — as it well might be — then heaven help us. It might all end in one mighty mass revolution to end all revolutions!

And if in the meantime you happen to see a poor little lost piggy with a curly tail and a black beauty spot at the tip of it — tell her to come home. Tell her I shall never again come anywhere near my poor little darling with any deodorant, shampoo — or even soap powder!

Those Monumental Trivia!

Have you heard that saying, 'Love me, love my chuckle'? — It says a lot doesn't it? Puts it, sort of, in a nutshell. All about us and that magic seventh sense, our sense of humour. And what a funny thing it is, our sense of humour. a joke can absolutely rock *me* with laughter, but all it gives *you* is one, big hippo-wide yawn. So very personal, so true of all humour. Which leads me to think that it's best to have friends with the same sense of humour as yours, so that your chuckle is your friend's chuckle too.

I hope that what makes me laugh makes you laugh too. And what makes me laugh? you'll ask. Lots of things, too numerous to list out here. But above all, what makes me hoot with laughter are all those monumental trivias about stars (the two-legged ones) and what fab fortunes they insure the various parts of their anatomy for.

Like legs for example. Did you know that Ginger Rogers, Fred Astaire's dancing partner, had her legs insured — guess for how much — for 40 million dollars. UN-believable!

Then invariably I would go into one of those higher maths operations: two legs 40 million, 1 leg 20 million — so how much would her one immortal big toe be worth? And that corn on that little toe? She must have had corns on her toes, for goodness sake, with all those marathons of dancing.

And those nail pairings — that's another thing. How come nobody thought of that? Somebody could have made a fortune on those big toe nail pairings. Packaging those nail pairings in some de-luxe packages, with 'Love from Ginger' tag, tied with yellow ribbon. A hundred bucks for ten toe pairings.

I often go on musing like that while in the kitchen, stirring my stew. Once I remember burning a whole batch of bread while working out how much Zsa Zsa Gabor's one eyelash would be worth if her two eyelashes were insured for a million and a half. Then naturally it got pushed to the absurd brink: how much to insure one lash of that famous eyelash?

However, I never worked this one out. Simply because — please don't laugh — I didn't know how many lashes there are in an eyelash, Zsa's in particular. By the time I woke up from this higher maths reverie all my bread was burnt to a brick of cinder.

The Ultimate — Laughmore
(Plastic) International

And now, my kindred spirit (non-bottle variety), I trust you
have saved a couple of teeny, weeny tears for our next
session of Misery Mona.

What am I going to moan about this time? This crazy
world of ours, fast getting crazier by the second, never mind
about the minute! Because, just look at it, Mamma Mia! It's
all gone plastic, hasn't it? Plastic bread and plastic sausage
and plastic heart and plastic flowers. Even laughter, you
know that? Even laughter has gone plastic.

You want a proof? Take a comedian on the radio, telling
you a joke. What do you get at the end of it? A human
giggle and a natural chuckle? The way you and I would
giggle and chuckle, spontaneously? Not a bit of it. All we
get is that synthesized, computerized and utterly
dehumanized . . . plastic racket. A raging roar of ha-ha-
has as if that laughter was coming from a giant can of some
Deodorant De Luxe. P-s-s-t, ha-ha plastic laughter.

And just now — I don't want to worry you — they'll be
canning laughter, like they can your beans in tomato suace.
What do you mean, how? Simple. Tape it. Rent a crowd
of a hundred yellers — all going ga-ga with ha-ha- and then
flog the jolly tape to four corners of the earth, that's how.
Then all they have to do is form a company with some
hifalutin hi-fi name like — Laughmore (Plastic) International
and, bingo, they'll make a bigger earkill than that genius,
Guglielmo Marconi did!

What do you mean it can never happen? It's already
happening. Turn any knob on your radio from Cape to
Cairo, Morocco to Milano, Outer Mongolia and back to our
Poffadder dorpie, and what do you get? Same old P-s-s-t
ha-ha plastic laughter.

And that's only the beginning. You know what will
happen next? With all this economising going on? All we'll

be getting is just P-s-s-t and no ha-ha whatsoever. It's already happening in America. Wait till I give you the latest buzz-buzz about this plastic biz-biz — it'll make you cry — my non-plastic friend. I promise you, cr--y!

But don't cry out all your tears. Save a tear or two for our next tearful instalment of our Misery Mona.

4

SQUARE EGGS

Me, Misery Mona?

Ah, please my friend, won't you be my KS — my kindred spirit — non-bottle variety? And lend me your ear for a moment or two? I so badly need a shoulder to cry on!

Because, really — some men, they are the utter end, utterest utter. Like my dearly beloved, my Macho Moustache, bless his macho moustache. You know what this funny creature calls me now? Misery Mona. I ask you — MISERY MONA! And — listen to this — he does it publicly now. Like the other day at the party. When he glibly declared, 'Come and meet my Misery Mona. She is going professional next month. Opening an office, Misery Mona UN-limited, International.' Well, I tell you, — I could have slayed him there and then with a peanut! Misery Mona indeed!

And all because now and again I moan a mingy little moan or two about this crazy world of ours! All right, three or four little moans. Three or four? cries my Macho Moustache — forty four more likely! And that — let me tell you — makes my continental blood boil 107 Celsius, whatever, in the shade — boil! And then I just let rip, rip till my moans spill, spill like beans out of a bag — all shapes and sizes. We need — I told him — 177 Misery Monas to do all the moaning that's needed to sort out this crazy world of ours!

And you know what he said to that? Grinning from ear to ear and gloating with glee. 'You don't need any other Misery Monas. You can do all the moaning for all those 177 — SOLO!

I am still reeling under that gleeful glee. What a thing to say! I dont know whether to laugh or to cry.

And now my kindred spirit (non-bottle variety) — I hope you've shed at least forty four tears. No, no, my friend, — don't count them now. Just let them drip, drip and keep on crying. Over this poor mistreated, misunderstood and

113

mis-everything else, Misery Mona. But don't cry out all your tears. Save a tear or two for our next tearful session of my Misery Mona.

Whatever Next — Square Eggs?

I don't want to worry you my friend, but you had better stop worrying about bombs in Belfast and bombs in Beirut and start worrying about this newest scientific bomb that's about to explode on our poor world any moment now — right under our noses.

What bomb? you ask. THE bomb, my friend. The bomb to end all bombs — the bomb in a form of a pea.

The scientists are about to produce a square pea, did you know that? That humble round pea that you and I put into soups and stews, that has been good enough in its perfect round shape for millions of years, ever since Good Lord has planted it in the Garden of Eden — that very pea is now being redesigned.

It all started back in 1985 when up popped this learned peaologist and decreed: A round pea is for the birds. For us humans it is completely non-functional. What we need is a square pea that will stay put on a plate and pack flat into those supermaket trays. And that's what the scientists have been doing. Crossing and re-crossing hundreds of mama peas and papa peas till now — Eureka! A square pea is about to be born.

Now — I know exactly what you are going to say. So what? It doesn't worry *me*. But wait till I tell you the rest of the story. This is only the beginning. Already the beanologists have straightened the runner beans. Another fellow tomatologist is working on tomatoes (oblong and knobbly), trying to produce a square tomato — again to pack flat into those square supermarket trays.

You can say miracles will never cease and chuckle over that. But all the same I can't help feeling, where is it all going to end? In a square bubble on your beer and square eggs? One friend chuckles, 'Why worry? It's all to the good. One day chickens are going to lay my favourite Scotch eggs (square) — already fried in deep olive oil.

Well — to that I am very sorry, but I am not even going to say: Ha, ha, v-e-ry funny. Because I am not a bit amused. The way I see it — the way all these -ists and -ologists are messing about with the shape of things in our poor world, I can tell you this now: Our eyes are not going to stay round for very long. Any day now, some bright spark of some -ologist will appear on the scientific scene and declare that our round eye is for the birds. That what we must have is a square eye to match all these mountains of square peas and square tomatoes and all those millions of square goggle boxes. And an eye will be born that will look like a cross between geisha's eye and an eye of some green robot from some outer space!

Me? Gullible?

Right now what I feel like doing is just letting my hair down and getting off my burdened chest all that's been bothering me for a long time. And what's been bothering me for a long time? Men, that's what, and my man in particular. Because, you know something, as he is growing older his head is getting bigger and bigger, till now — I am not kidding — he fancies himself as a regular, resident headshrink, for ever telling me what's wrong with me and my alter ego.

In his latest headshrinking session it was me, the gullible goose. The other day he declared, 'You forever cry how gullible other people are, but you are just as gullible. If you want to believe that pepper is the best cure for sneezes, you will believe in it and no Prof. Barnard would ever persuade you otherwise.'

Me? Gullible? Really!

It all started during one of those nice little spousely natters when you always start with kings and invariably end — nobody knows how — on cabbages. Anyway, this time it was all about all those weird cures for all sorts of rheumatism that some people believe in. Like, tie a string of seven garlic cloves (peeled) round your neck and you'll be cured of rheumatism for ever. Or sprinkle a cent's worth of flowers of sulphur into your bedsocks and you'll never feel a rheumy twinge again. Or do what Monty, my bridge partner does. He wears a copper bangle round his ankle and simply swears by it.

We went on happily chatting and chuckling over all those weird cures till we finally came to our good friend, Serah Simkin, whose magical cure is — guess what? A nutmeg. Put one nutmeg into a muslin bag, tie it just above your sore knee and that's it — you got yourself a miracle cure. 'You know, really,' I cried to my husband, 'our Serah is a regular nutmeg case!'

117

And that's exactly where we got 'stook' — if you know what I mean — on this nutmeg case. Because straight after my darling headshrink said, 'And you? You are a potato case?' Well, I tell you — this was like a proverbial spark set to a ton of tinder. 'Me — a potato case?' I fumed. 'Just because I once rubbed a slice of potato into my sore elbow?'

'You did?' chuckled the brute.

'I did and I admit it,' I told him, 'but what you are forgetting is what I did with that potato. I didn't tie it round my elbow, did I?'

'No,' he agreed, 'you didn't. But,' he argued on, 'the mystery still remains: What exactly is the difference between a nutmeg and a potato?'

'A w-o-rld of difference,' I cried, 'because a nutmeg is just so much dead and dried up exotic dust, good only to dust up common bread pud, with no vital juices whatsoever. While a potato — you know yourself — is alive and oozing with enzymes, with all those vital juices. That's the difference. In fact, ever since that magical cure for my elbow, I always keep a potato handy in my make-up case. And, I tell you something else — I am seriously thinking of writing to Prof. Barnard, telling him of my wonder cure for his arthritis.'

'Your only problem is,' said my headshrinking brute, 'that Prof. Barnard has many cases, but he hasn't got a make-up case.'

My Elixir Of Youth

I am a lucky old girl, endowed by Providence with a bottomless supply of chuckles, provided by my dearly beloved old 'square' — bless his for ever 'square' heart!

Recently he has developed an all-consuming passion for health foods and fads and so last Saturday he brought home — wait for it — a kilo of . . . buckwheat.

'Buckwheat?' I cried, my eyes like a couple of saucers, 'I thought buckwheat was for chicks and bucks only!'

'N-o,' cried my dearly beloved, 'buckwheat is a Russian rice. And you know what it says on the packet here? What buckwheat can do for you? For your brain, heart and arteries. Rejuvenate your vital innard, my girl, completely. Now I ask you, who could resist an elixir such as this "youth for ever" rejuvenator?'

Not me, but, sad to say, we hit upon a big snag in this rejuvenation adven-choor. The snag being the indisputable biological fact. That we humans are not bulls and cows with three stomachs to digest rock-hard buckwheat husk — however rejuventating. So we simply had to mill the stuff somehow, and I tell you, you'd laugh your head off if you saw us doing it.

'Homogenizer!' we cried, 'That'll do the trick, de-husk.' But all the homogenizer did was to whirr and whirr and w-h-irr, worse than Pop Shop. Till I cried in despair, 'Stop it! I'd rather stay geriatric forever!'

We then tried our little hand-turned, thimble-size nut grinder which takes just about fifty seeds to fill it. So, after a single hand-turn we cried, in unison this time, 'That'll take us till 2.500!'

And so, in the end — oh, please don't laugh — you know what we were reduced to — the rolling pin. And back to the Stone Age. Taking a handful of the stuff and rolling it on and on with the rolling pin. Then blowing away the hard husks — and I suspect half the elixir of the eternal

119

youth with it. Because, you know what — all we got in the end was about ten grams left out of the whole kilo!

So here is my advice to all elixir hopefuls and all prospective buckwheat lovers of the world: Start hating buckwheat forthwith and pronto!

Oh, To Be Cheese Smellologist (Chief)!

2001 A.D. roll on — chop fast! So that you and me could emigrate to some saner climes on some distant planet. Because, really, this crazy world of ours is getting crazier by the minute!

Take just this one crazy craze: competitions. Do you know I've counted sixty three in six days — sixty three! Every time my weary eye rests on a page, there is a bleary competition screaming at me: Enter now! Guess a number of peas in a pod/matches in a matchbox/sheets in a roll (baby bottom soft) — I ask you!

Nine out of ten I do manage to resist, but there are always one or two that this poor little sucker, me, falls for and ends as — you've guessed it — a flat-footed flop.

Like I fell for this 'Match 10 Famous Nostrils with 10 Famous Noses' competition. Didn't win a bean, but my family is still ragging me : what have you matched Ma? Sophia Loren's nose with Pope's pontificial nostril?

My latest — and most exotic — flop was a competition for a cheese smellologist. What fired my fiery imagination was that GOOD TASTE TEST, remember? When three famous glitterati were invited to test that glorious gourmet veg: Pea in a Can.

Soon after there was this entry form, saying: 'Have you a discerning nose? Can you tell the difference (blindfold) between gorgonzola blue and rat-trap cheddar? Write in 50 words how your nose can promote our Chew-n-Chew Cheddar?'

'Promote?' I wrote. 'Are you joking? With my Say Cheese Smile in seven and a half languages (the half being Urdu), I can charm a cheese hole . . . out of a cheese hole, and with my talented nose for exotic odours and aromas — I can beat, no bragging — all the chefs and Escoffiers of the universe. In short, I can sell your entire production with just one single sniffle of my phenomenal snozzle!'

121

But, alas — there was a strangest twist to this cheese hole tale. The computer must have spewed my entry form in hundreds and sent it to all the other world cheeseries. Because, weeks after — guess what — I received a letter from the Alpine Goat Cheese Corporation, Berne, Switzerland, saying: 'The entire production 1988-1998 has been sold. And from 1998 to 2008 our production will be taken by our technological marvel, Cheerio Cheddar, a microchip cheese. No holes, no smell no-cheese cheese.'

That's the trouble with this rotten world — it doesn't appreciate real talent.

Help, Plastic Caviar's Coming!

Our Misery Mona (she of the 4,000 moans) says:

I don't want to worry you my friend, but it's about time you started worrying. In fact, it's well past the eleventh hour fifty nine minute mark. Because, just look what they are doing to our food! And I don't mean us popping food pills or licking some French Fried Ice Cream fantasy. I am talking facts, my friend — some fearful and frightening food facts.

Did you know, for example, that your bread — already tasting like boiled mattress — is about to be made from formaldehyde — a gas and coal derivative? And your steak will soon be spun from plastic protein threads, like your knickers are on machines; and that — right now, the Brits are testing synthetic foods (plastic to you and me) made of trees, oil — and don't freak out! — manure; and that the French are turning crude oil into frogs' legs, coq au vin and that gourmet's delight, Porca marmelada?

Your mind boggles, doesn't it, as your tummy turns. And, on top if it all — listen to this — they have the cheek to call all this plastic junk semi-synthetic. I ask you. Semi? In my book semi means half. Now which half do they mean — I'd like to know? When even that gourmet delicacy, caviar, now comes like your toothpaste, in those squeeze tubes. Honest to God — caviar! And the ad brazenly declares: This tube caviar has nothing to do . . . with caviar. Can you beat it? Next they will brazenly brag: Your steak has nothing to do with . . . steak and your bread has nothing to do with bread!

You may well ask, where is it all going to end, all this universal plastic junk conspiracy? I tell you where. They'll turn us all into X kgs of solid plastic, that's where. You don't believe me? then go on, by all means, and merrily glutton yourself with all that plastic junk and you'll see. One day you'll pinch your arm and you'll prick your arm and you'll

123

pierce it with a ten inch needle and there won't be a squeak of an ouch, there'll be just a kilo and a half of solid pink plastic!

It can't happen, you say? You want to bet! Why do you think all those sci-fi Star Wars glamour girls all look like plastic dummies? Because they are. They are what they've been fed on. Plastic bread and plastic steak and plastic caviar.

It scares me plastic-stiff. I can see myself one day pricking my funny bone with my chuckle pin and my funny bone will be all gone pink plastic — and dodo-dead! For now — till my next moan — I wish you happy moaning!

Can You Believe It — Edible Papers Next!

Remember my last maxi moan? About plastic food and those weirdie foodologists, bless their weird bald pates? Concocting all those gourmet yum-yummies. Like frogs legs and coq au vin and Porca Marmelada out of . . . crude oil and cooking gas and manure, of all things! That was my first instalment.

And my second is: you know what I'd L-O-V-E to do to those foodologist? Send them all, you know where? To the moon — on a one way ticket!

Because, you know what the loony breed has invented now, on top of the above yum-yummies? The ultimate in lunatic concotions this side of the twenty first century. Ultimate enough for you and me to throw up and freak out. And the invention is — don't freak out —*the edible paper*!

Can you believe it? The edible paper! I mean — have a heart! It's bad enough to read your sex and scandal rag let alone to chew it! The report says (a copy will be gladly supplied to all doubting Thomases and Thomas-eses, £100 + tax): the edible paper process separates fibrous cellulose from nutritious glucose, adds various yeasts, moulds and bacteria and eureka! You have a quality protein, already being tested as feeding pellets on Merino sheep at Waka-Nooka, Western Australia. And you know what that means — a couple of research projects on? What we will be getting next? That last Sunday sex and scandal rag you threw with disgust into your waste paper basket will now be converted into a de-li-cious Vienna Shnitzel à la Sunday Rag!

And I can see, can't you, what will follow next. A culinary revolution, no less. When your recipe will say: finely chop up your *Howick Advertiser*, add three cups of water and mix it to a paste; add three Ann Landers columns, chopped and fried; then grease your pan with a page of any oil advert, pour the mixture in and there you have it. A delicious newsprint Omelette Supreme!

125

I can't help crying, 'Whatever next?' There seems to be no limit to those next 'whatevers' — does there? Because, you know what — just below that Edible Paper bit there is another title: Your Next Dehli Delight — Your Swimming Pool Algae for Your Scrumptious Breakfast! Nightmares never cease, do they? But more about that yum-yummy delight in my next unmerry moan!

Help — Plastic Breakfast Is Coming!

Some people are so ungrateful! Here is me, poor Misery Mona, moaning my tongue out of my head, trying to warn the world that: plastic steak is coming! And plastic caviar in a tube is coming! And plastic frogs' legs are coming! And what do the people do! Form street demos, carrying placards: Down with plastic frogs' legs? Not a bit of it. Instead, you know what they do? They moan at me. You are moaning again! — I ask you.

Jealous, that's what they are. In case I win that coveted The Moaner of the Year Award, which — humbly I brag — I well might. Because this time I have really scooped the scoopiest moan in my entire Misery Mona career. Now — you know that loony breed, the one I'd love to send to the moon, on a one-way ticket — that one? The perishing loonies are at it again. and you know what they've concocted now? Out of that green, slimy algae in your swimming pool? Plastic breakfast. Gospel truth, cross my Christian heart and my future pacemaker — PLASTIC BREAKFAST!

So hear ye, hear ye, whoever has ears to hear; plastic breakfast is coming! According to the report we already have juicy steaks made of feathers, straw, wool and hair and delicious pies made of petrol waste. And now for the latest: by next Christmas the Food 2000 Corp., USA, will have perfected the ultimate: a Synthetic Breakfast, S.B.11. This — swallow hard now — this will combine the chemical composition and the flavour of bacon and eggs, toast and marmalade in a four-in-one combination. All you have to do, madam, is throw a slab of S.B.11 on your frying pan and you'll have a dream of a yum-yum breakfast.

My mind, *she* boggles and my tummy it turns. And are they going to de-kipper my kipper too? To go with the de-marmaladed marmalade? And what will happen to our poor farmers now? They'll all go bankrupt and no kidding.

Because I mean, with an onslaught of such culinary delicacy, a mish-mash of bacon and eggs, toast, marmalade *and* kipper — our poor bacon and eggs doesnt stand a smell of a chance!

But, alas, this crazy world remains as stone deaf as those Stonehenge monstrosities. And as for my Macho Moustache — I am shocked by his reaction. I perorated and I thundered and I waved 'Plastic frogs' legs are coming' evidence right under his moustache, but not a hair in his moustache as much as quivered, once. Un-real!

Spare a Tear for Next On the List — Plastic Beer!

This is a four-hankie weepie from me, Misery Mona to you,my Kindred Spirit, (non-bottle variety) — four-hankie weepie! But first to re-cap. You know my current bee under my moan-moan bonnet? Plastic food. And how I try to save the world from oncoming onslaught of plastic frogs' legs and plastic hot dogs and so on and so forth.

But alas, — this crazy world is stone deaf to all my prophetic prophesies. And so, as a last resort, I naturally turned to my Macho Moustache, hoping that at least I can stir HIM to some dy-namic demo action. Like carrying my dream placard saying 'Down with plastic frogs' legs!' and 'All Plastic Legs — go home!' slogans.

Vain hope. All I got was 83 kgs of C.C.L (Couldn't Care Less!) — with a moustache on. There he was, sprawled like a lord, his feet up, a beer mug by his side, absolutely dead to the world. And even dead-er to all plastic legs and me. Chewing, guess what? His favourite chewing gum for the eyes — his sports page. And you know what that was? I have since spied on it. Los Paraguayos v. Los Uraguayos match; and which Amigo kicked whose shin at Las Metros stadium, millions of kilometres away — can you believe it?!

'Don't you ever care?' I perored, 'this poor world is going to plastic hot dogs and other plastic legs, fast — and you don't care a hoot about it! Really, — it's enough to turn my stomach, the very thought of it!'

It didn't turn my Macho's stomach though. In fact, it didn't turn a single hair of my Macho's eyelash — left or right. His both eyes kept chewing on about those Los Amigos at that . . . Las Metros.

Which, — as you can well imagine — made my moan-moan hobby horse go ga-lloping crazy. 'You know what you are?' I cried, '83½ kgs of C.C.L (Couldn't Care Less) slob, — with a moustache on. Those plastic legs would have to perform a nightmare and walk up those jolly stoep steps, for you to stir, sir!'

And you know what the brute did? Lifted his eyelids a slit, peeped over the edge of the paper and said: 'Till such time, when they do walk up those stoep steps, do me a favour. Be a good girl, and let me enjoy this mug of beer in peace.

'Uh!' I cried, flopping into my Goma-Goma chair, 'they'd have to turn your beer into liquid plastic beer, before you take any notice.'

For once I give up — till my next moan.

Spinach Lovers of the World Unite!

I don't know how many of those learned gents called scientists are reading this and being a gentle lady I'd hate to upset them, but really, enough is enough.

Did you know for example that the scientists are spying on spinach and dissecting its gourmet beauty something c-r-uel? Up to date they have found 000,01 nitrate (poison to you and me) in it and are now looking for another 0 so that they can ban this delicacy from your menu forever.

To a spinach lover like me this is sacrilege. I wish they'd stop. I wish they would find themselves another moon to explore, so that they'd stop spying and snooping on my vegetable basket — and my spinach in particular.

The thing I have against these -ists and -ologists is this: for centuries untold millions of us ordinary folk have lived and thrived on vegetables of all sorts. Now, all of a sudden — millions of spinach omelettes after — along comes this smart-ist of a scientist and says, 'Don't you believe a word they tell you about vegetables being good for you. Because they aren't. Some of them are quite the opposite — full of poison!

'And,' he croaks, 'I don't mean food additives or colorants or contminants either. I mean actual food. Our actual food contains thousands of toxic substances. Take a look at the list: onions, turnips, radishes and cabbage all have toxicants causing goitre; spuds have solanine, tomatoes lycopine, bananas dopamine and beans and almonds cyanide. And that means p-o-i-son.'

As to spinach, this learned gent says, spinach is a fraud. It contains too many nitrates (whatever they are) and these nitrates can be converted by bacteria into nitrItes (whatever these are) which can cause anaemia — in babies in particular.

Spinach *causing* anaemia? When for decades we all believed it *cured* it. Really. If Popeye lived he'd just keel over and die — his spinach biceps and all!

I suppose at a pinch I could cut out all these foods on the list — and live. But what about all those that are *not* on the list — as yet? And what are the scientists going to spy on next? Because, rest assured, once they start they won't stop till all the bugs are banned — friends and foes alike.

Like the bugs and bacteria in cheese, for example. There must be a gold mine of them, in all those holes. Just imagine what's going to happen next, when they get their spy-specs on that jolly lot. That'll be the end of my beloved Gorgonzola, I bet.

And I bet they won't stop there either. Just looking for 'holes' in cheese holes. They'll be looking for holes in toad-in-a-hole and in Yorkshire pud; in bubble 'n squeak and in my yeast macaroons. Everything and anything they can lay their spy-specs on. Till you and I will be too scared to look at the food, leave alone eat it. We'll just have to stop eating, stop eating altogether.

My husband laughs. 'Isn't that what you have always wanted? Haven't you always been saying, ''If only I could stop eating, I'd be s-o happy!'' Now you'll have your wish — and a perfect diet!'

V-E-R-Y funny!

5

CHRISTMAS
AND
NEW YEAR

Jumbo Christmas Headaches
For The Ultra-rich

Our Misery Mona (she of the 4,000 moans) says:

Right now you are fretting your poor brain to a frazzle, worrying how to buy seven gifts with the money enough for three and what to buy Aunt Nellie and Cousin Katie that you haven't bought two Christmases before and oh, forever sighing, 'If only I had that million bucks, all my worries would be over!'

If that's what you think, then you don't really know what money worry is. For money, my fretting friend, is like that saying about children, remember? Small children small worries, big children big worries.

I know you won't believe it, but the more money you have, the bigger your money worries. Only whilst you and I fret about 100 bucks and where is it to come from, our poor millionarie worries about his $100.000 and what is it to be blown on. Now which is bigger — your 100 or his 100.000?

Some of their worries would curl up your hair like no Wella perm ever would. My American missionary friend says in America the papers are full of eccentric Christmas headaches for the ultra-rich. Forever worrying what gifts to blow their millions on. Domestic robots or midget submarines? Chastity belts or gold toothpicks? Egg decapitators or fig leaves for statues? Elephant leg spitoons or meat choppers with the mink-trimmed handle. Imagine it! Fretting yourself daft, worrying whether your wife would love (passionately) an elephant leg or would prefer mink-trimmed meat chopper. Give me those unsexy socks for my Macho Moustache, any time!

And don't forget, those Mr Big Cigars have millions of worries how to guard their millions. Some of them agonize which latest in bodyguards they must buy for Christmas: a python or a croc to guard their families. One Greek shipping magnate gave his teenage daughter a twelve foot black zigzag python . . . to be kept in a cage in her bedroom. Imagine going to bed with a monster like that at the foot of your bed! Uh, the very thought of it!

Or imagine the heebie-jeebies poor Lady Docker must have gone through when she was given, of all monsters, a tame croc to guard her swimming pool. Now that, I tell you, would turn me into a creep-crawly human reptile in five seconds flat!

I could go on till next Christmas — all facts and no fiddle. All this to warn you that if by next Christmas you win a cool million, don't think for a moment you'll have no worries. Take it from me, you'll have millions of worries you never bargained for. Meanwhile Happy Worrying!

Hooray — Christmas Is Over!

Phew! Am I glad Christmas is over! Because boy oh boy, the problems I had with this universal Yuletide loving and all this 'everybody must love every creature on this earth — including cockroaches' business. Now, how can this poor little mortal me love the whole universe and all the cockroaches in it? Honestly, it's enough to give you an inferiority complex!

See my problem? And the reverse of this was even a bigger problem. When they started loving *me*. All the shops I mean. they never seemed to stop . . . loving me. I reckon they must have started this Christmas 92 'Love me' promotion the moment they stopped the Christmas 91 'Love me' promotion. Till come Christmas I felt absolutely exhausticated with all this Yuletide loving!

Do you know, I've had enough 'We love you' Christmas cards from all sorts of strange shops — to plaster a shop. Some of them the funniest ever — cross my Christian heart. Like a pussy card for a cat I do not possess; and a doggie card with a plastic bone glued to it; and a kiss-kiss card from the Fragrant Plastic petunia Company, and another — the prize of the bunch — 'We love you' card from the Mini-Bini-Kini Bar, with a loving PS: Come and see our lovely range of mini-bini-kinis. me, who can't get into granma's bloomers 42 size — I ask you!

But the one that took the Christmas cake this time was the one which said, We'd love you to come and choose a loving tombstone for your darling, sadly departed husband. That was the last straw. A tombstone for my husband! That's alive and kicking — and how! After that I got so cross I went tearing and shredding all these Yultide lovelorns like a shredding robot gone berserk!

But Fate, alas, has a way of teaching little know-alls like me what happens when a mere mortal tries to be too clever by half. Because soon after I was having a quiet tête-à-tête with my lovable self on the stoep, when my dearly beloved asked, 'Where is that envelope that came yesterday with a cheque for . . .

'Never mind what for and how much,' I cried 'just get me a stiff whisky!

Macho, Just Stop Breathing — That's All!

And now you will ask, What's my moan, this brand New Year? Unmerry moan, my friend, very unmerry. Right now I am planning to fit in a nervous breakdown, as soon as I get over these wretched — just torn up — New Year Resolutions. Because, uuh, this yearly self-torture is driving me up the wall — and not slowly either!

You should have seen me last night. In front of my mirror, my mascara drip-dripping and me mop-mopping over poor me — the floppiest flop that's ever flopped!

My ever present Comic Imp chided me with his usual tongue-in-cheek glee: And you know why you are the floppiest? Because you are too selfish. Only thinking of your own self-improvement. Why don't you start improving other people, for a change? You'd make a fortune writing resolutions for other people's Anno Dominis. Sell it in hundreds, 50 cents a piece. Who wouldn't pay that to spare themselves the agony of that yearly ritual. So get cracking and write resolutions for other people. For all those twits and dimwits that steadily drive you up the pole. Like bank tellers and pool attendants and shop and office assistants and tax and garage men — and traffic cops and such creeps. And one for your Macho, of course . . .

'Of course!' I cried. 'Why didn't I think of that? Of one for my Macho. Boy, oh boy, have I got a list for him — that long! Of millions of 'musts' and trillions of 'mustn'ts.'

So here are some of the thirteen (my lucky number) 'musts' of my first trillion:

1. He must never ever say: You never ever . . .
2. And never say: You al-w-ays . . .
3. And most of all never say: I didn't say what you say I had said, that time you say I had said, whatever you say now that I had said. Because I didn't say THAT! You did. It's you who said that I said . . . This particular 'never ever' is one of those mind boggling marital

perennials that sends this poor little feeble female reaching for a rolling pin, I tell you, quicker than you can say: Roll on pasta fasta!

4. He must stop his nightly musical — his 'steam engine' snore; must either have his poly-lipops or whatever burnt out of that shnozzle of his or else go to sleep in the dog house. Where he can join his fellow Super Snorer, Fido — to perform their nightly Grand Snore Symphony.

5. He must ban, banish and abolish that jack of all sounds, that hundred-in-one monosyllable he mutters a hundred times a day — all right, ninety nine times — called H-m-m-m. And replace it with HOW. Example: HOW fascinating, exciting and a-b-s-olutely thrr-i-lling is your yap-yap, even if it's about nail varnish on your big toe (left), darling . . .

6. He must learn by rote how to say I LOVE. Example: I love that lumpy custard, that burnt toast and all that left-over mishmash of your culinary disasters . . . darling . . .

7. He must learn how to spell 'sorry' (yes, like little Johnnie spelling sorry, sorry, sorry) and thereafter say 'sorry' everytime he opens his mouth. Seventeen times a day, — even if only one sorry is justified. And the other sixteen? He'll be paying me back for all the millions of 'sorries' he owes me in arrears.

No doubt, somebody else's Macho will cry: But that means your poor Macho Moustache would have to stop breathing, more or less.

My answer to that is: No more or less. Just stop breathing!

Down With New Year Resolutions!

You want to know how I feel about all these New Year jubilations? Lousy. That's how I feel, absolutely lousy. In fact, right now, this brand new month of January I feel so down in the dumps I could cheerfully drown myself in my own swimming pool. Just plunge in and never plunge out. Yesterday morning, I tell you, I felt so desperate that I actually went right to the edge of my swimming pool and gave the water a quick feel-see test with my big toe — but the water, I regret to report — was far too cold to drown in, I mean for me to drown myself in comfort.

And it's all about that perennial headache, those wretched new Year Resolutions. Because year in and year out doggedly I would write my twenty point resolution and then doggedly I would stick the copies of the jolly old screed all over the jolly place: my fridge, my desk, my cooker, my bedside table — only to find that I break these resolutions, I tell you — I break them quicker than I make them. Year after year after year.

It's like some macabric self-torture ritual, forever doomed to fail. Because count for yourself: twenty years at twenty resolutions a year, what does it make? Four hundred resolutions. And half a tone of waste paper and half a forest ripped getting it. And where are they all now? On the municipal dump, that's where.

And even more to the point: where has it all led me? Precisely nowhere. After all this trying everything under the sun and blaming everything under the moon. Hot and cold weather, sun and moon spots, atomic bomb, even rock punk (pink) — you name it, I've blamed it. If after all that I am still as bad as ever, then I resolved, I must end it all — now. Get myself a bottle of plonk, drain it to the dregs, then plunge myself into eternity via my swimming pool.

But you know something — believe it or not — even that was the resolution that never was. Because just as I was giving the water another quick feel-see test with my big toe for the fatal plunge, my Comic Imp inside me stepped in to commiserate with this poor desperado.

'Cheer up', it said, 'there are millions like you all over the world. Instead of all this moping and plunging and plonking, think what a benefactor you are. The paper mills, for one thing, must be making a fortune milling all this waste paper pulp for the municipal dump. What would they do without you? Or for that matter KWV and Stuyvesant and Nestles. What would *they* do if you and people like you stopped smoking and drinking and guzzling? They would go bankrupt, wouldn't they?'

'And lastly,' my Comic Imp chirped on, 'think of it this way: if you, say, made *one* good habit a year, there wouldn't be any room for any bad ones by now, would there? And you would have nothing to moan about, would you? And that being your favourite occupation, wouldn't that be absolutely tragic? If you became perfect. Imagine it! You'd be a perfect paragon, perfectly Unbearable, Unlovable and Uneverything else, with not a soul of a friend in this whole wide world. For who would want to be friends with a perfect freak like that? So — give up all this giving up and stop all this 'give up this and give up that' and instead start laughing at yourself — for a change!'

Ha, ha — very funny!